ALF COBB
MUGSBOROUGH REBEL
THE STRUGGLE FOR JUSTICE
IN EDWARDIAN HASTINGS

MIKE MATTHEWS

THE HASTINGS PRESS
PO Box 96 Hastings TN34 1GQ
hastings.press@virgin.net
www. hastingspress.co.uk

First published 1991.
Republished by The Hastings Press, July 2003.

Acknowledgements

1991 edition: With thanks to Roger Povey and the Hastings Library Staff.
2003 edition: With thanks to the Fishermen's Museum, Hastings, for the portrait of JWE Chubb, and to George Chubb of Burlington, Canada, for information on his grandfather.

Front cover: Alf Cobb in 1910.

Set in Garamond.
Typesetting and cover design by Helena Wojtczak.
Printed and bound by Antony Rowe Ltd, Eastbourne.

In Memory

of

Alf & Polly

Alf Cobb at the time he stood for
election to Hastings council in 1910.

Book Review

ALF COBB: MUGSBOROUGH REBEL

A fascinating new book written and published by a local man throws fresh light on both the history of Hastings and of the national labour movement.

Alf Cobb: Mugsborough Rebel, by Mike Matthews, tells the story of a London street hawker who transformed Hastings politics in the first decade of this century. But he also had a much wider and more profound impact through his friendship with Robert Tressell, author of the *Ragged Trousered Philanthropists*. Tressell's novel, set in Edwardian Hastings (Mugsborough), has been acknowledged by generations of labour leaders as one of their most important sources of socialist inspiration. Now Mike Matthews has saved from obscurity the key individual influencing Tressell's view of life and politics at that time. Alf Cobb came to Hastings from Hackney in 1900, bringing with him his baby daughter. He set up home with a local flower girl and earned a precarious living, mainly as a street hawker and costermonger.

This was a time of great poverty and hardship for many of the residents of Mugsborough. Unemployment grew rapidly through the decade. Large crowds of jobless men gathered at the Memorial every day, sometimes going on marches round the town begging for food and money.

Cobb suffered as much as any of them, and determined to do something about the inequality and corruption he saw everywhere around him. He soon became the leader of the local branch of the Marxist group called the Social Democratic Federation, drawing large crowds to the regular open air meetings where he condemned the system that had created so much suffering.

Cobb attracted the attention of the local press through his repeated revelations about corruption in the town hall and the local establishment. He also took legal action several times to defend the interests of the ordinary ratepayer. Luckily these dramatic events, and many of Cobb's fiery speeches, were recorded in detail in the newspapers at the time, and Mr Matthews quotes extensively from these in his book.

'Cobb was the archetypal rebel,' said Mr Matthews. 'Through his quite remarkable wit and blazing defiance he was able to outmanoeuvre the inevitable reactionary backlash. He survived innumerable attempts to place legal constraints against his trade, and was bankrupted, imprisoned and sued for libel'.

The book follows Cobb's extraordinary career as a political firebrand through to his election as a councillor in 1921, followed a few months later by his sudden death from war wounds.

Alf Cobb: Mugsborough Rebel paints a vivid portrait of both a fascinating man and a decisive period in the history of Hastings.

STEVE PEAK

HASTINGS & ST LEONARDS OBSERVER, 27TH NOVEMBER 1991

PREFACE

This book attempts to combine a comprehensive social history of Hastings with a chronicle of the adventures of a notorious resident – Alfred J. Cobb. Its contents cover the years 1900-1921, thus incorporating the Edwardian era; the period in which Robert Tressell wrote his celebrated *Ragged Trousered Philanthropists*. Both men were close political colleagues and members of the Social Democratic Federation.

Whilst Tressell played only a minor role in the S.D.F's organisation, committing his energy to writing one of the great Socialist novels, Cobb became its inspirational leader, quickly propelled from virtual obscurity as a mysterious, unknown ex-Londoner, living under a variety of false names, to branch secretary of the Federation.

Alf Cobb deliberately set himself up as a public muckraker to uncover the truth behind allegations of corrupt local practice. The scandals represented in fictional form by Tressell had a solid factual basis; many being rooted out by Cobb with the assistance of Corporation employees acting as informers or 'moles'. In Edwardian Hastings, Cobb was renowned as a mob orator of exceptional talent and audacity. He was the automatic choice of his S.D.F. comrades in local debate or public address. As his political flame burned brighter, so the outrage against him spread. He was never immune from police surveillance and harassment. The story follows his long running, often hilarious battles with the town's authorities as they unsuccessfully fought to contain his growing influence over 'Mugsborough's' working class. Some of Cobb's most witty speeches are recorded, helped by the extensive reporting of the time. His letters to the local press, always sharply humorous, are also included.

Cobb was the archetypal political rebel. The local vendetta against him never slackened. He was bankrupted, constantly dragged before the Borough Bench, imprisoned, and sued for libel in the High Court.

The War Years of 1914-18 are also documented, together with the peace celebrations and post-war period up to Cobb's premature death in 1921.

Lastly the book highlights Alf Cobb's irrepressible spirit and inspired humour that saw him through years of poverty and political oppression. Hastings has seen no one like him since.

MIKE MATTHEWS, 1991

CHAPTER 1

ALF COBB'S EARLY YEARS IN MUGSBOROUGH

This story begins in the closing days of the Victorian age. The century had turned and the twelve months that followed would dramatically transform Alf Cobb's life. At the start of 1900 he was in London, a respectably married commercial traveller; by the year's end he was in Hastings, living apart from his wife, working incognito for a secretive drapery concern.

Alfred James Cobb was born on May 23rd, 1874 in Hackney. His father, John William Cobb, was a baker with strong Socialist sympathies. Both father and son became staunch members of the Independent Labour Party soon after its formation in 1893.

Before Alf's sudden move to Hastings, the Cobb residence was in South West Hackney. His wife, Florence, a small-time London actress, gave birth to their second child on May 30th 1900 at the family home in Appleby Road, London Fields. The new daughter was named after her mother and known always as 'Florrie'. Only a few months were to elapse before the marriage broke up. In those times, because of the comparative high cost, divorce was restricted to persons of moderate means. Alf Cobb's fluctuating income based insecurely on commission prohibited that option. For the majority of the years that lay ahead, Alf carried the social handicap of being legally married but physically separated from his wife. It was not until the onset of the Great War that he finally obtained a divorce to marry his long time sweetheart, Polly Bassett.

The most extraordinary feature of the separation was Alf and Florence's joint decision to split up the family. Their elder son remained with his mother while Cobb left for Hastings with his newly born daughter in his arms. There is no doubt that he was settled in Hastings with Florrie sometime before December 1900. That month he was summoned to appear before the local County Court after damages had been claimed because his horse had backed a trap into a resident's window. Earlier on, a Hastings doctor twice called on him to vaccinate his baby daughter. Alf was to recount, years later, how the doctor was 'courteously denied the pleasure'. He had read of the large numbers of children dying from the effects of vaccination. Should Florrie contract a childhood disease, he preferred to chance that she would fully recover. More remarkable is the fact that when Alf brought the infant Florrie to Hastings she was less than six months old.

The main consideration in breaking up the family was probably to share the financial burden. This would also allow Florence to pursue her stage career. And so it was that Alf and Florrie arrived in Mugsborough approximately one year before Robert Tressell. For the first year they shared a house at 17 Brook Street with a friend of Alf's named Charles Spinks. Best guess is that it was Spinks' wife that nursed and cared for Cobb's tiny daughter. Alf was busily occupied in his new position as secretary for a drapery firm called Thompson and Co. Immediately he became entangled in the intrigue and duplicity of the firm's two shady owners. Alf Cobb took on the role of impostor; by sleight of hand the unknown outsider became Alfred J. Thompson, draper.

His appointment as secretary at Thompson and Co. establishes the first link in the chain connecting Alf Cobb to Robert Tressell and the characters depicted in *The Ragged Trousered Philanthropists*. But why did Alf become so closely identified with a draper's shop to the extent that he was listed as A.J. Thompson in a local street directory? Who were the two business owners desperately anxious not to reveal their identities? What purpose was there in muddying the waters by encouraging a newcomer to adopt a false name? Both of the firm's owners were prominent Hastings businessmen. One was William Laite, a liberal Councillor, who edited the *Hastings Chronicle* and published the *Weekly Mail and Times*. The other was Frederick Bruce, Mugsborough's leading ironmonger, with shop premises in Queens Road and York buildings. On all accounts Bruce had an abysmally wretched reputation as an employer. By an odd coincidence Robert Tressell was to work for Bruce at his shop in York Buildings in 1901. The experience had a profound and sobering influence on Tressell and strengthened his radical political consciousness.

Opening a new drapery business, operated on credit, would entail open competition and rivalry with other long-standing firms. In Tressell's novel it was 'Adam Sweater' that led 'The Forty Thieves': 'He was always the chief, although not always Mayor,' writes Robert. Significantly, in the book, Tressell identifies Sweater as the managing director and principal shareholder of a large drapery business: 'in which he had amassed a considerable fortune.' In Edwardian Hastings the only individual that combined both positions was Charles Eaton. He was a leading draper and Town Mayor in 1904. So if Adam Sweater was in real life Charles Eaton it is no wonder Bruce and Laite were determined to keep their involvement with

Thompson and Co. quiet. Charlie Eaton was not to be crossed at all cost.

Whatever the truth Alf Cobb did not survive long at his secretarial post. At some stage he either quit or was fired. He may have grown tired of the deception or clashed with Bruce. But more likely the business was losing money and he was given notice. An additional problem for Bruce was his partner's poor health. Laite was suffering from nervous exhaustion through overwork complicated by a lung disorder. A specialist recommended an extended sea voyage to Australia or South Africa. Bruce abandoned any further sharp practice and transferred the ailing business to share part of his wide shop front in Queens' Road (now Discount Heating Supplies). Laite, safely abroad, was no longer in a position to offend the future Mayor, Charles Eaton. Both were members of the local Liberal Party. The transfer failed to save the drapery firm and by 1904 all trace of 'Thompson's' had disappeared.

In June 1905 Harry Houdini was drawing huge crowds to the Hastings Hippodrome. He was the greatest attraction ever seen on the local variety stage. Frederick Bruce was eager to share in the limelight and challenged Houdini to escape from a large hamper that was to be locked, strapped and roped. To save face the Chief Constable had refused to lock Houdini up in the police cells. He easily escaped from Bruce's hamper and from a straitjacket supplied by a Hastings 'lunatic attendant'.

During his employment as a secretary, Alf had met a young flower seller by the name of Polly Bassett. She was well known in the Old Town circles as a firebrand and rented a house in Bourne Street. She quickly became his mistress, working companion and 'mother' to Florrie. She left the slums of Bourne Street and moved in with Alf. They set up shop together, conscious that gossip over their affair, if widely broadcast, would severely damage trade. Mugsborough was renowned for its small town, stifling morality. Polly and Alf remained inseparable. She was always fiercely loyal and supportive; death alone parted them.

For a short period they ran a florist shop behind East Parade but it was not a success. They traded under the names Thompson and Bassett. Only doors away stood the large wholesale greengrocer's 'Southern Produce Co.' Alf was briefly employed by this firm in 1903 and it later supplied the credit, in September, 1904, to enable him to open his own greengrocer's shop at 10, Norman Road, St. Leonards. This time he was known commercially as 'Paul Bassett', possibly at his creditor's insistence to avoid any scandal. Maybe the florist's had closed because their relationship had been discovered.

In October 1905, Cobb brought a man named Miles into partnership, trade was poor and Alf struggled to supplement his earnings by hawking fruit and vegetables in the street. Eventually Miles took over full responsibility for the shop while Cobb was forced to spend many hours as an outdoor vendor. One day Alf returned to find the shop closed up and all the stock removed. Heavily in debt he re-opened the greengrocer's hoping business would improve in the summer months of 1906. But trade did not revive and Cobb went bankrupt.

The Bankruptcy Hearing was held in September 1906. The Court was curious to know why Cobb had used the name 'Paul Bassett'. 'The simple reason was that of the two of us, Miss Bassett was perhaps the best known,' responded Alf. This deflected questions about his personal life. He and Polly had lived above the greengrocer's shop in Norman Road.

The background to Cobb's greengrocery failure forges another link to the events described in *The Ragged Trousered Philanthropists*. Amongst the 'Brigands' was one Amos Grinder. Tressell wrote that Grinder 'had practically monopolized the greengrocery trade and now owned nearly all the fruiterers' shops in the town'. In the novel, he was managing director and principal shareholder of the company concerned. He was, in Robert's words, a self-made man, cunning and ruthless. Should Mugsborough's retailers refuse to purchase their foodstuffs from Grinder, he would open branches close to a recalcitrant greengrocer and sell below cost.

In Hastings, circa 1900, Paine, Rogers and Co. monopolized the wholesale and retail greengrocery trade. There is very little doubt that 'Amos Grinder' was modelled on Stanley T. Weston, Chairman and Director of Paine Rogers and Mayor of Hastings in 1906. If the pair have been correctly identified, Adam Sweater was based on Charlie Eaton and Amos Grinder on Stanley Weston – Eaton and Weston. Significantly, Tressell gave the name *Easton* in his novel to a painter employed by Rushton and Co.

The connection between Paul Bassett, greengrocer, alias Alf Cobb, Socialist and Councillor Grinder, infamous member of Robert's band of brigands rests on the ownership of Southern Produce Co.: the firm that briefly engaged Alf's services and later supplied him with goods on credit for his shop. The company director was F. Rogers – Southern Produce was an offshoot of Paine Rogers.

But it is hard to believe that Rogers chose ruthlessly to drive Cobb out of business; after all, his company was supplying Alf with fruit and vegetables on credit. Cobb's indebtedness and bankruptcy was Rogers' loss.

By 1913 the shop premises that Alf and Polly had vacated at 10 Norman Road had been absorbed into the much larger premises of Adams and Jarrett, builder's merchants and undertakers. When Robert Tressell left his position at Burton and Co. in 1906, he was taken on at the Adams and Jarrett workshops in Alfred Street, St Leonards. The builder's merchants transferred their business to Norman Road in 1910 and extensions demolished Cobb's old greengrocery store three years later. In Tressell's book, Adams and Jarrett is re-named 'Rushton & Co., Builders and Decorators'.

In desperation the bankrupt Cobb turned his thoughts to the emigration escape route. He had received a tempting offer of employment as a market gardener in British Columbia from a former Hastings émigré. Only lack of cash stopped him from paying his passage. He applied without any luck to several organisations for the necessary funds. Finally he made an application for assistance in emigration to the Hastings Distress Committee in January 1907. He proposed to take little Florrie, then aged six-and-a-half, with him. His application could not include Polly Bassett. His application form stated that he hoped to repay the grant out of his basic wage plus a percentage of the market garden profits. The application for assisted passage was never seriously entertained. Any prospect for his emigration bid had disappeared when a Distress Committee member asked his colleagues: 'Would it not be breaking the law to assist an undischarged bankrupt out of the country?'

Cobb was destined to remain in Mugsborough. In years hence many of his political enemies would have willingly paid for his 'transportation' out of their own pocket. He may have fallen on hard times economically but his political star was on the rise. Within the space of twelve months he would emerge as the pre-eminent figure in the Hastings Social Democratic Federation.

Alf Cobb and Robert Tressell joined the Socialist movement on the same day but there were vast differences between the two men. Alf had been encouraged as a youth to read the works of Marx. He strongly believed in a Socialist system wrought by social change. His political instinct adhered to the practical step by step objectives of the Independent Labour Party. Cobb possessed a down to earth pragmatic faculty. He searched relentlessly for immediate remedial measures to help his fellow working man and the mass ranks of unemployed always conspicuous in the old, economically blighted Cinque port. He regarded Robert Tressell very much as a visionary.

Tressell, in contrast, was more the revolutionary idealist. He dreamed of the overthrow of capitalism with a greater passion and emotional intensity. While Cobb led from the front – organising branch meetings, challenging opponents to public debate, standing for municipal election – Tressell stood aside, watching, listening and recording; horror-struck and fascinated by Mugsborough's misery and degradation. Both men complemented each other.

Alf Cobb was outgoing and self-confident. He had a rare talent as a political agitator. It made him a marked man. Checks were made on his domestic circumstances and background. Local Tories discovered, in 1908, that he had been placed on the borough's voting list as Alfred Bassett. They lodged an objection and Alf's vote was disallowed. The following year, in September 1909, he applied for re-instatement at a Revision Court hearing. At that time Polly and Alf were living together in a house in Middle Street. As evidence, Cobb produced the previous year's rent book to show that he was the tenant rather than Miss Bassett. The Registration Solicitor's suspicions were raised.

'How do you keep your 1908 rent book so wonderfully clean?'

'Well, I was born in 1874 and I am still clean,' replied Alf.

'That's different; you don't wash a rent book.'

When Cobb was unable to produce the 1907 rent book, the Revising Barrister expressed disbelief in many of Alf's earlier statements. 'If you have a mistaken view of things, I have no control over the views you choose to take, although they may be mistaken and entirely unwarranted,' said Cobb. 'I never expected you to find the 1907 rent book.' 'In that case,' retorted Alf, 'don't you think you are wasting my time and your own time and the time of all these gentlemen here, by asking me to produce this rent book, when you are sure I shall not do so?'

'It is quite possible you are right as to that,' admitted the Barrister, closing his book with a bang.

The sitting was resumed the next day. The Revising Barrister opened by saying the whole case had caused no end of trouble, with Cobb the chief culprit. The rent book, in evidence, had been 'got up' for the sole purpose of bringing it before the Court; it was quite obvious many of the entries had been made the same day. He told the Court that not even Mr Cobb's landlord had known his real name, believing his tenants were man and wife. During the last six or seven years Cobb had used two other names apart from his own – Mr Thompson and Mr Bassett. In the last two rate books the person listed at 52 Middle Street was Mary Bassett. 'I disclaim any responsibility for the gross ignorance or crass stupidity of the Overseers in calling me Bassett or for the foolishness of the people of Hastings in knowing me as Thompson through my connection with the firm,' replied Alf indignantly, 'the only reason why they refuse to put me on the register is because I go to work in the wrong way. If I had treated the Revising Barrister in a confidential manner and smoothed him over as Liberal and Tory agents did, I would have been on the register now.'

'I will not have you use that language,' replied the Barrister, angrily. He sternly rebuked Cobb and advised him to leave the Court.

'Oh, I am going now,' responded Alf perkily, 'but I am going to state my views first.' Alf Cobb stalked out of the Court. The Barrister disallowed his claim. After the hearing Alf wrote a letter of explanation to the local press indicating:

> That a prominent political agent informed me in the Revision Court that my claim would have been passed had I treated the Barrister differently. Another agent stated that one political party was as much in the mud as the other to keep me off the voting list. Why?[1]

His association with the failed drapery business had lingered on into 1906. Rate collectors had persisted in issuing demand notes to him under the name Thompson.

The Revision Court hearing provides some clues into Cobb's life in Hastings. He acknowledged, for instance, that he had lived at 52 Middle Street (the house is now demolished) since the latter half of 1907 and that he had earlier opened a fruit shop in Queen's Road under the name Bassett.

When his emigration hopes were dashed in 1907, his heart was still set on earning a living as a small shopkeeper. He opened another greengrocer's; this time in Cross Street, St. Leonards. The shop soon closed. Destitution and the Mugsborough Poorhouse beckoned. One alternative lay open – to take his fruit and vegetables onto the street and sell them from a barrow. He became a street trader and for the majority of his remaining years in Hastings worked as a fruit and vegetable hawker and periodic commission agent.

CHAPTER 2

MUGSBOROUGH – A STUDY IN POVERTY

The years between the onset of the Twentieth Century and the outbreak of the Great War were years of desperate hardship for the bulk of Mugsborough's labouring classes. Over the period 1899-1913 economic historians have estimated that real wages fell by about 10%. The general fall in living standards depressed the already dwindling local holiday trade. As Cobb wrote in 1907:

> Hastings is a non-industrial town, which depends entirely upon visitors for its prosperity. Forsaken by our wealthy classes, we must rely upon the tripper, or short holiday class. The only occupation that might be classified as an industry, fishing, was itself in decline.[2]

Once the tourist trade slackened off, many working men's families watched with apprehension the approach of winter when building and construction work came to a standstill. Then numerous skilled workmen, especially carpenters, bricklayers and painters were laid off to join the burgeoning levels of unemployed, swelled by the summer season's casual labour.

Because Hastings had no industrial base it lacked any tradition of organised trade unionism and collective support. The development of mutual aid and working class solidarity was greatly restricted and working men were at the mercy of unscrupulous employers. Wage-slavery and oppressive working conditions flourished. There were accusations that the Corporation sweated its labour force ignoring the fair wage clause written into every employee's contract.

Discounting his wartime service overseas, Alf Cobb lived in Hastings throughout the first two decades of the new century. He sought a precarious livelihood as one of 150 local costermongers who worked the streets as 'barrow boys' or basket sellers. Winter was a lean time for the street hawker often reducing the numbers by half. In the winter months the outdoor traders struggled to placate their anxious creditors in the hope that losses might be recouped in the summer season ahead. With trade in recession shopkeepers strongly opposed the existence of the street sellers describing the hawker as 'a trading bird of passage' making no contribution to the upkeep of the town. Cobb disagreed, insisting the majority were lifelong residents of Hastings.

Many of the bleakest examples of wretchedness and privation were found in the Eastern Hastings districts of Halton and Ore together with areas of the Old Town, including the slum infested Bourne Walk (known today as The Bourne.) One day in December 1902 an Old Town Wesleyan pastor fiercely spoke out. He made an impassioned appeal for funds to aid the poorest members of his congregation whose only income was four shillings per week parish relief. He calculated that rent reduced this amount by half a crown leaving a pitiful remainder for light, firing and food. The pastor was unshakeable in his opinion that a desperate amount of poverty existed all over Hastings, sometimes obscured by 'a frantic effort to keep up appearances'. He wrote:

> Let it be remembered that in Old Hastings the only appearance which is kept up is that which corresponds to the grim reality of poverty and hunger – at this moment I am visiting those who are sick, the doctors urge nourishment: they might as well urge the moon.

Winter charity concerts were organised to provide Old Town children with boots and shoes; cast off boots and garments would be gratefully accepted. Soup kitchens were re-opened. Large numbers who applied for relief had neither coal nor food in the house, In January 1904 a local journalist observed:

> A long procession of women with haggard faces, poorly clothed and some with little children toddling beside them wearing boots and shoes which for a long time had not kept out the wet waiting outside the Grove Road Mission Hall, Ore.

A month later the Ore Relief Fund subscription list was almost entirely exhausted and applicants in the West Hill district were refused relief. Hungry looking children were to be seen with jugs and cans anxiously waiting outside the soup kitchens for the appointed opening hour. Two hundred would gather daily at the Sandown Road council schools for the Ore Penny Dinners. At these dinners they would receive their only square meal for the day; each child was allowed as much soup, bread and jam as he or she could devour. On January 8th 1904 two thousand poor children were feasted in the Public Hall at the invitation of the Delvanti's Operatic

Society. For many children it was the first substantial meal they had eaten for some time. Their clothes were in a filthy state; the half jackets tattered and torn, many wore nothing but a coat and trousers and a rotten pair of boots without a sole, heel or toe. Hastings journalists recorded that the spectacle was a truly pathetic sight. Remains of the feast were placed into bags and handed out to several poor women standing outside.

Common lodging houses abounded in the Old Town where the homeless poor could obtain a night's shelter for 4d. Another alternative to sleeping rough was to seek accommodation in the Workhouse casual ward. The Workhouse was so jam packed with itinerants in 1903 that an urgent request was issued for twenty-four new bedsteads. These were placed in the dayroom. The wandering traveller could spend a temporary night's lodging at the Mendicity Society House in Roebuck Passage. The menu consisted of a supper of soup and bread and breakfast of cocoa and bread. Nine or ten itinerants could be sheltered here each night. On average 1300 wandering tramps made use of the Mendicity House each year. The annual grant provided by the Corporation to this Society amounted to a miserly £20 in 1904.

That year a local newspaper reported that scarcely a week passed without a large batch of respectable working people being hauled before the Borough Magistrate for non-payment of rates. Some cases had to be adjourned as the defaulters were already in prison, incarcerated for previous rate defaultment.

Poor people had a natural aversion to begging for 'relief' from the local Board of Guardians. In July 1906, a child's body was conveyed to the Borough Cemetery in a sack and buried without religious ceremony. This 'Pagan' burial caused a minor scandal. The anguished mother was heard to cry out that her child was buried like a dog. The acting chaplain was harshly maligned by fellow passengers as he travelled to the Cemetery by tram. An anonymous correspondent complained that:

> The poor at death are compelled to display their poverty to the world either by accepting the pauperising aid of the parish or the scant ceremonial they can provide themselves...
> Let any reader stand as I have done at the door of an elementary school on a winter's morning: let them observe the pinched faces and the scantily clad forms of many of the little scholars and let them find if they can a dog which exhibits such palpable evidence of cold and hunger.

It is nearly certain these bitter words belong to Frank Willard, Secretary of the Hastings branch of the Independent Labour Party. In 1911 Willard launched a savage assault on the local Education Committee:

> If it were say – the Corporation horses which were being worked in a diseased state, the matter would be different and the Councillor who dared neglect them would be held up to public scorn and denounced as an unfeeling monster. But then horses matter and these are only children. And yet look at this child, a puny mite of six years. She is not clothed. She is merely covered. A something, neither my wife nor I can tell what it is, is rolled and tied around the top part of her body – for the lower part she is covered with a small skirt of flimsy stuff that you could blow peas through. Yet mite as she is, she is sensitive and tries to hide her stockingless and otherwise unclothed condition. She has discharging eyes, the lids of which are red and inflamed and she suffers from a chest complaint. And let it not be thought that she is an exception. She is but a type of hundreds. Others at school are in such a badly booted state that they had better be barefooted – many of them must have perpetually cold and wet feet. Is it a wonder that at the first cold snap the school attendance is decimated or that whooping cough and other illnesses prevail among them?

One day in the Spring of 1902, the Chairman of the Housing Council concluded that the sooner a working man with a family emigrated to somewhere outside the town, where he could find employment for his children, the better. The 1910 Census underlined the serious problem of emigration facing the Borough. The town's population total of a fraction over 61,000 was 7000 fewer than expected. Hundreds of residents were leaving Hastings each year.

They fled from hunger and destitution. No other town on the South Coast of comparable size lost such a high proportion of its inhabitants to Canada and Australia. A spokesman for the Sussex Colonising Association confirmed this unprecedented mass exodus in April 1911: 'considerably more people have left the town recently than ever before'. Their passage was assisted by the Central Aid Fund, local Distress Committee or Board of Guardians. By 1913 Mugsborough residents, in record numbers, were making a wild dash for Canada. Young men were spending their last penny to get out. Not surprisingly the largest numbers of emigrants came from the poorest districts of Hollington and Ore. Rumours spread that a whole street was virtually emptied by emigration.

Suicides in Edwardian Hastings were commonplace. Scarcely a week passed without the local newspapers recording a resident's death by his own hand. Tressell came to view Mugsborough's self-inflicted deaths as 'ordinary poverty crimes'; essentially these were society's crimes. The means varied. Cliffs, railway lines, rooftops and high windows were all deployed for this grim purpose. Some cut their own throats; others threw themselves into a rough sea or drowned in Alexandra Park's reservoirs. In September 1907, a Hastings man, James Loveday, was found drowned on the beach at Bexhill. He had been unable to find work and the police had refused to allow him to play his whistle-pipe in the streets. Loveday, near starvation, had walked into the sea.

The cost of renting a typical workingman's dwelling took a large slice of the family income. Local railway employees could find their sixteen-shilling wage packet reduced to four shillings after the landlord called: the station porters were unpaid and survived on tips. Few artisans secured a decent home unless they paid more than a third of their wages on rent and were obliged to sublet. Visitors frequently discovered houses in Ore had a family living to each room. Other dwellings had a bed in every room including the kitchen.

Houses in the Old Town, particularly in the vicinity of The Bourne, were wholly unfit for habitation and ought to have been condemned long before the slum clearances of the 1930's. The newspaper correspondence of Henry J. Hunt, in the summer of 1920 tells of the multitude of hovels and bug hutches which infested the town:

> Many houses in Hastings are horrible hovels: old, insanitary and disgusting; quite unfit for chicken houses let alone men, women and children. I have seen in some homes bugs hanging from the four walls of the rooms in clusters as large as the top of a teacup. On tearing the wallpaper some fell on my feet, a revolting sight. These things for years have permeated the walls of these hovels called houses until even if the housewife be as clean as she will, she has an almost overwhelming task to get rid of them.
>
> These haunts ought to have been done away with years ago and yet some of these same homes… are regarded as picturesque, beautiful, something to elevate one's mind and thoughts to look upon. Visitors would rather look down on the huddled mass of bricks and tiles, bugs and worm-eaten woodwork, narrow passages and thoroughfares with their cramped-in hovels breeding filth and disease and aiding all kinds of degeneration which should disgust any kind of civilised being. What real good can it do the town to be able to point out some old tumbledown place as the reputed birthplace of some celebrity? How many discharged soldiers

with their wives and little ones are there compelled to live in these abominable places? I should think it makes their blood boil. Fancy the year 1920 seeing houses with four or less small rooms with sometimes sink and copper in the kitchen. No bathroom, leaky roofs, but little or no back yards and with from six to a dozen or even more persons forced to live in them. I have known some of their little children having to sleep on the shelves of the kitchen cupboard and being bathed in the copper.

If those landlords, some of them with honoured names, could be sent to prison, who weekly extort rents for these hovels, often with the aid of the most bullying agent they can find and yet will not spend a penny to put them in reasonable repair, there would be a stir, I'll warrant.

Hunt had visited, door to door, some of the worst slum areas of Whitechapel, Bethnal Green, Shoreditch and Hackney without finding conditions to compare with the narrow streets and passages of the Old Town. He believed a clean sweep was required:

To condemn a house here and there was quite insufficient. Shame on you gentlemen who have to sit in Council for many years until your hairs are white and allowed these things to continue. Some of you are among the hard landlords drawing rent and profiting by the horrible conditions. How many have been driven to drunkenness and then brought up before a shameless landlord magistrate and perhaps sent to prison, a place the landlord richly deserves?

For two weeks in January 1907, a unique event occurred in the history of Hastings. Hundreds of unemployed artisans and labourers marched in organised processions through the town to raise funds and solicit public sympathy. Fronted by a brass band repeatedly playing the same mournful tune, the men tramped daily often for five hours at funeral pace behind a large banner that read 'In aid of the Genuine Unemployed'. As each day passed the length of the procession grew. Four or five hundred men would trudge slowly past the residential and 'aristocratic' districts of St. Leonards. Small placards worn sandwich fashion asked for donations for the several collection boxes. They would muster at the Drill Hall, Middle Street, Station Road or Wellington Place to form four abreast and pass silently and gloomily along the seafront to deliberately cover the most fashionable thoroughfares, returning to share out the day's collection. This might average from 1s 5d to 1s 10d per man.

The greatest pity and financial support was shown by the lower classes rather than the wealthier and comfortable inhabitants. Servants' pennies would rain down on the procession as it passed the large houses along the Marina or Upper St. Leonards. Not until the band rested did the onlooker appreciate the sadness and depression on the marchers' faces. Many of the thousand male unemployed would watch in the crowd. These spectators were equally in urgent need but too proud to ask for assistance.

Alf Cobb and his Social Democratic Federation comrades disapproved of 'begging' marches. As Socialists, they demanded not charity but the right to work.

Leaders of the I.L.P. adopted a less rigid line. They sponsored three further parades in the first week of December 1907. They were on a smaller scale, more disciplined and tightly controlled, mustering on average barely a hundred men. The processions were led by officials from the I.L.P. behind a man of giant stature named McPherson. Only those who had registered their names with the Distress Committee were allowed to take part. This was to rebut past accusations that the marches had attracted every rapscallion and undeserving loafer to be found. Any man seen smoking was asked to leave the procession. Officials agreed, after consultation with the Chief Constable, to limit the number of parades; the unemployed would march only in sufficient frequency to ensure their distress was not forgotten. The organisers even bowed to the police chiefs ruling that the unemployed should not enter Christ Church on Sunday morning to join the congregation. The marchers reluctantly complied and covered the return distance from the Fishmarket to Bopeep.

Chief Constable James showed little sympathy for the destitute unemployed. When, in August 1908, a group of Midland Hunger Marchers reached the borough border at Bulverhythe, they were met by a detachment of police and prohibited from travelling along the seafront. They unsuccessfully remonstrated against this decision for over three hours, loudly cursing the Hastings police as blacklegs and blackguards before being directed to a rear route via Boscobel Road. They had tramped from town to town along the South Coast dragging a horseless four wheel van piled full of progressive literature. Declining the 'prepared hospitality' awaiting them at the Hastings Workhouse, they elected to camp for the night off Sedlescombe Road North, close to where the Old Pottery had formerly stood. The hunger marchers enjoyed a supper of bread and potatoes washed down with water, in obvious preference to the local Workhouse diet. They had cleared out of Mugsborough by morning, moving on to Winchelsea and Rye.

CHAPTER 3

THE NATIONAL DEMOCRATIC LEAGUE

Alf Cobb became branch secretary and acknowledged leader of the Hastings Social Democratic Federation in July 1908: rather less than two years after it was formed. The decision to establish a local branch of the Federation sprang directly from the disintegration and collapse of the Hastings National Democratic League.

The arrival of the socialist movement in Mugsborough was long overdue, considering the prevailing social conditions and economic distress. Ironically, when the Hastings N.D.L. was set up, nationally the organisation was sinking into oblivion.

The League had blossomed briefly after the General Election of 1900 in the doomed hope of uniting Radical Liberals, Labour and Socialists into one large democratic body for the common good. David Lloyd George had been one of the original supporters. Its initial momentum derived from widespread hostility to the campaign in South Africa, popularly known as the Boer War. Once the war was over, the League lost its political bearing and gradually faded into obscurity. By November 1905 its total membership had shrunk to under seven thousand.

So by the time the Hastings branch was formed in February 1906, at a crowded meeting in Ore, the League was in rapid terminal decline. Some indication of this general slump in support is given when a visiting Peckham executive committee member mentioned that London looked upon Hastings as one of their liveliest branches.

Frank Willard was the leading architect behind the branch's formation and was appointed secretary. At the opening meeting he described the new branch as a rampart against reaction, an incentive to progress and a step towards the sovereignty of the people. But Willard's early enthusiasm quickly waned. The Hastings League was judged to have made a bright start but in the space of a few months, a damaging split emerged between a Radical Liberal faction and the vast majority of the Committee who were ardent socialists. This deepening rift made it impossible to construct a coherent programme of action or function as a cohesive unit.

Little of this brewing discontent was manifest at the outset and the membership continued to grow reaching at best over a hundred. John Ward, M.P. for Stoke on Trent, addressed the first mass meeting at the

Public Hall in April and J. E. Dobson, general secretary of the Democratic League, was invited to speak at two outdoor meetings in July. Harry Courtney, a staunch Brighton democrat, addressed two open-air meetings that summer.

The guest speaker that followed Courtney onto the League platform was H. Pay, a well-known member of the Tunbridge Wells Social Democratic Federation, the most active branch in Kent or East Sussex at the time. Pay was an old friend of Robert Tressell and had once worked in a baker's shop in Robertson Street. Placed on an employers' blacklist, he was compelled to leave Hastings and seek his living elsewhere. By 1906 he was residing in Tunbridge Wells and was connected to the Socialist Sunday School movement. Other members of the Tunbridge Wells S.D.F. made appearances as guest speakers including W. G. Veals, branch secretary, who addressed two rallies in August and September.

The preponderance of Social Democratic speakers arriving in Hastings at the invitation of the League Committee, dominated by socialists, did not escape notice. Eventually a local member proposed that the Hastings League should become a branch of the S.D.F.: 'if we have socialist speakers let's become affiliated to the Federation and sail under true colours'. This suggestion disclosed the concern of the Radical Liberal members over the League's leftward drift. Socialists, on the other hand, were discovering that the League, far from being an independent democratic organisation, was merely an advanced wing of the Liberal Party. Its main objective – the representation of labour and democracy upon on all elective bodies – 'did not go far enough' for Frank Willard and his socialist colleagues. Willard had keenly studied the progress of the Independent Labour Party in the House of Commons. In September 1906 he informed the League that it would have to dispense with his services; he wished to work independently and dissociate himself from both main political parties. Displaying a customary arrogance, he announced that he would place no obstacle in the way of the formation of a branch of the S.D.F. in Hastings.

Willard also made clear that he had accumulated disturbing evidence showing that subtle pressures were being brought to bear on some of the more prominent Socialist N.D.L. members. He cited instances of victimisation where the livelihood of members was being jeopardised by their connection with the League. Orchestrated attempts to disrupt local branch meetings had occurred. For some months Willard had written anonymously a regular column for a Liberal weekly outlining the League's progress. These are his final observations:

We have had to seek the aid of Socialist speakers who have come free of charge, sometimes charging less than railway fare and by these means we have been enabled to make our programmes continuous. Moreover there are many regular attendants at our meetings who regard the N.D.L. as a party organisation and will not join it on that account, but who would join either the I.L.P. or the S.D.F.

Under these circumstances, aggravated by the frankly anti-socialist attitude of some of the League's speakers, it was inevitable that a rupture would come: socialists are not going to carry on a propaganda for some other party. If they work for any cause, it must be their own; and this is why there is a demand for an avowed Socialist organisation. And as my sympathies are with the Socialists it is with them I shall throw in my lot.

This review summed up the shortcomings of the N.D.L. for local Socialists. There is no indication that either Alf Cobb or Robert Tressell ever considered joining the League, well aware of its ties to the Liberal Party.

As the League began to slide into an insignificant force the core of its active membership joined the Social Democratic Federation. Frank Willard was swift to act after his resignation. He penned a short article in the S.D.F's national journal *Justice* requesting all Socialists in Hastings and its immediate neighbourhood to communicate with him. The first mention of a new Hastings branch is made in the *Justice* issue of November 3rd, 1906. Willard was incorrectly described as secretary. Perhaps he regarded himself as corresponding secretary but he was never officially appointed. The post of branch secretary went to J. M. Kerr.

The Hastings S.D.F. branch was founded during a period of major Socialist advance throughout Sussex. The S.D.F. Brighton branch had been successfully revived in March 1906 and a large educational meeting was organised there in May. Representatives of S.D.F. and I.L.P. branches and Clarion Fellowship Assemblies from Kent, Sussex and Surrey met in Eastbourne on July 29th. They formed the South Eastern Federation of Socialist Societies and five hundred people were present at the demonstration and speech that followed. It was agreed to 'swop and obtain speakers and open up new spheres of activity'. Some of the founder members of this new Federation were drawn from the Hastings Clarion Fellowship and other Hastings socialists also attended. Regular Social Democratic Federation meetings continued in Eastbourne as the S.E. Federation expanded its influence. Thus the political environment was particularly favourable for the emergence of the S.D.F. in Mugsborough in the month of October 1906.

CHAPTER 4

SOCIALISM UNVEILED

The opening public meeting of the Hastings Social Democratic Federation took place on Friday, October 12th at 'Ye Olde Beehive Dining Rooms', 32 Pelham Street. The dining rooms were run by a Mrs. Lewcock and named after a forceful weekly national Labour journal from the 1860's sympathetic to Chartist aims. Before Friday night's gathering at Mrs. Lewcock's two small discussion groups met at the Cricketer's Public House.

There was a good attendance at 'The Beehive' and it was unanimously decided to form a branch. F. Owen was voted to the chair after it was agreed that, rather than making a permanent appointment, a Chairman should be appointed from meeting to meeting (Robert Tressell borrowed the new Chairman's name and called the hero of his novel Frank Owen.) Apart from J. M. Kerr's appointment as Secretary, a J. Hutchings was nominated treasurer. The new branch had the full backing of the South Eastern Socialist Federation and George Meek, its Secretary, travelled from Eastbourne to address the first open meeting held at the Fishmarket.

As a movement of national importance, the Social Democratic Federation had a stormy history. Originally associated with Radical workingmen's clubs, it was founded by Harry Hyndman in 1881 under the name 'Democratic Federation' and only adopted its full title in 1884 as its programme shifted towards a revolutionary brand of Marxist Socialism. Its wide ranging political programme attracted many diverse left wing groups into its fold – anarchists, socialists and social revolutionaries – elements that caused bitter internal wrangling and gave the organisation a turbulent and chequered career. Remembered today as Britain's first Socialist political party the S.D.F. survived an endless succession of splits and traumas to eventually merge with the Communist Party in 1920.

In Hastings Charles Harrison notified the *Weekly Mail and Times* of the inaugural branch meeting, defiantly challenging the Editor to publish their views with honesty and fairness: 'we local Socialists have sufficient belief in the strength of our doctrine to hold out against all comers either in public or in the press'.[3]

Both Alf Cobb and Robert Tressell were present at the first branch meeting. Cobb brought into the S.D.F. a small collection of Socialist students; members of an educational group he had organised to study Marxist political theory. This was the exception since the education of the vast majority was restricted to board school.

From the outset no love was lost between Alf Cobb and Frank Willard. The dislike was mutual and soon turned into a public display of personal hostility. The reasons are not difficult to unravel. In Fred Ball's published work on Tressell he describes Willard as an irascible but very able man. As a Christian-Socialist Willard had always championed the cause of political radicalism from a moral and humanitarian standpoint. He had learnt that Alf Cobb was a married man living openly with a mistress. The knowledge affronted his puritan sensibility.

In his book *One of the Damned* Fred Ball narrates details of an incident at Phelps Coffee House where Cobb was requested temporarily to leave a S.D.F. meeting held soon after the branch's inception. The majority of members considered his affair with Polly Bassett should not be allowed to bring his expulsion from the branch. Ball is certain the decision in Cobb's favour led to a split in the Social Democratic ranks. He believes that this breakaway group, headed by Willard and a moral minority, quit the S.D.F. to launch a local branch of the I.L.P. It is doubtful, however, if the formation of the I.L.P. branch in April 1907 can be entirely attributed to antipathy towards Alf's extramarital relationship. There's evidence that many of Frank Willard's S.D.F. colleagues thought his conduct priggish and authoritarian.

Willard wished to stamp his authority on the rising socialist movement and play a dominant role in the direction of its political activity, in the same way as he had controlled the N.D.L. Although not elected in any official capacity, he regarded himself as the S.D.F.'s de facto leader. Already Willard had wrongly informed *Justice* that he was branch secretary, even forwarding the branch's first report, signed F.H.W. His report relates how 'Comrade' James Thompson had organised the local unemployed marches: 'today "Thompson the Socialist" is one of the best known men in Hastings.' Alf Cobb strongly repudiates these claims one week later:

> Thompson is not a 'comrade' of the local branch, he having refused to join us because our opinions and rules are too strict. He was chairman of the N.D.L., which has breathed its last in Hastings. Willard is no longer a member of the S.D.F. His resignation three weeks ago was accepted with pleasure by the branch.

Cobb gave two reasons for Frank Willard's resignation:

> One, he was trying to get the S.D.F. onto Tory and Liberal candidates committees in the recent council elections. Two, he had tried to wreck the branch because people had curbed his autocratic powers.[4]

Alf Cobb was convinced Willard was behind the anonymous correspondence that had rubbished the S.D.F's attitude to Municipal trading:

> I have no doubt the writer is Mr Willard, who, I may say, has been a member of other organisations than the S.D.F. Those persons who were then fellow members with him and who are not members of the S.D.F.; on hearing of his resignation from our organisation, warned us to look out for squalls. We of the S.D.F. do not mind squalls, as long as we are attacked fairly, but we certainly must object to his misstatements which appear in your columns.

Cobb maintained that Willard did not attend S.D.F. meetings frequently and denied that any member had ever observed that Municipal trading was synonymous with Socialism. His reply was a crushing rebuke. In the letter he defines Municipal trading 'as at present conducted, to be more beneficial to the well-to-do classes, inasmuch as Municipal control of gas, water, telephones, markets, etc., are all run on Capitalistic lines for the purpose of profit. He continues:

> Mr Willard often refers to Karl Marx and twits the S.D.F. members with either not having read his works or with having forgotten them. Mr Willard is extremely fortunate to have been able to purchase them and afterwards to spare the time to read, and moreover, understand them, but here allow me to say that membership of the S.D.F. is not denied to those who have not been able to tackle Marx or even to those who have failed to agree with him, but it is open to anyone, male or female, Christian or otherwise, who believes in the 'complete emancipation of labour from the domination of capital and landlordism, to be replaced by the Socialisation of the means of production, distribution and exchange'.

> Yours truly,

> Alfred Cobb,

4 Banks Cottages,
Hastings,
26th January, 1907.

P.S. I hope Mr Willard, when marching with our unemployed on Thursday last, saw the irony in the men composing that procession having 'Britons never, never, never, shall be slaves' played to them for a marching tune and them with an empty stomach. Did he also unite in giving three cheers in Wellington Square after the National Anthem was played? I trust Mr Willard will use his time to better advantage, by educating his fellow-townsmen to provide employment in future and so put a stop to the recurrence of another winter exhibition of poverty in our midst, point out the causes and its cure, and then Mr. Willard will be doing something more lastingly useful than by endeavouring to discover mistakes in the S.D.F. which do not exist.[5]

The public feuding and rivalry between the old leadership of the League, Willard and Thompson, and the resolute upstart and 'young pretender' Alf Cobb had reached a new pitch. James Thompson read Cobb's sarcastic comments on the unemployed procession. He joined the public slanging match:

I am glad to say that as a result of our parades the matter of finding work has been pushed forward and today, in several hundred homes there are fires in the grates and at least something on the table, where had the matter been left to the S.D.F, cheerless homes and hungry children would have been. If I were a member of the S.D.F. I would hide my head in shame at my branch's inactivity instead of trying to cover up its deficiencies by paltry excuses.

P.S. Since writing the above I hear that Mr Cobb has informed the world, through the London official paper of the S.D.F. that the Hastings branch of the N.D.L. is dead. Well, it played a pretty good part in the unemployed parades for a dead organisation and seeing that it has about three members for every one on the books of the local S.D.F. it is a fairly healthy corpse. Mr. Cobb mistakes its present silence; it is simply resting.[6]

Thompson was not mistaken. The S.D.F. took no active role in the organisation of the unemployed marches. Its policy was to abstain from direct involvement because it considered the parades were structured on a basis of charity rather than the principle of the right to work. But the local branch bombarded the Town Hall with communications demanding action to reduce unemployment. James Kerr, branch Secretary, sent the following letter to the Council at the beginning of February 1907:

> I am instructed by the Hastings branch of the S.D.F. to call the attention of the your Council to the great number of men, who, owing to the causes of unemployment are parading the thoroughfares of our town daily. We venture to point out the small financial support being given to the 'Distress Fund', it being totally inadequate to meet the vast amount of distress prevailing and would urge the Council of the necessity of using their power to enforce the halfpenny rate, believing it to be the duty of the Council to deal directly with this very serious question of unemployment as we consider it a disgrace to our town that the alleviation of the distress in our midst should be left entirely to the public who are charitably disposed.

Kerr's communication intensely irritated the Councillors and drew a ludicrous outburst of invective from Councillor William March – who had once moved that the N.D.L should become a branch of the S.D.F. An Alderman asked that Kerr be informed that the halfpenny rate could only be applied to emigration and clerical expenses. March urged the meeting that the clerk should in future be instructed to refrain from printing such material on the agenda: at meeting after meeting they had received communications from that 'assembly in Pelham Street' and the agenda was constantly loaded up with such correspondence. Kerr had been told before that the Corporation had no power to levy the rate. March compounded his ignorance by accusing the S.D.F of 'forcing itself on parades and wished to give them a political character, which could only end in disaster to the unemployed.' He was sure that the generous public would never have made the liberal response if they had any idea those taking part in the parades were Social Democrats:

> I know that body well. It has had three secretaries within as many months. It meets in a little coffee shop in Pelham Street and is an association without any followers. The reason they had written is to gain a little notoriety by having their communications in the press and on the agenda.

The socialist response to March's false charges was penned by an anonymous 'Social Democrat'. The language is witty and contemptuous and bears the hallmarks of Alf Cobb:

Councillor March and some of his confreres feel annoyed that the Social Democrats should have the audacity to take an interest in their own municipal affairs. They object to us bombarding them with notices and resolutions in regard to their shortsightedness and indiscretions in the management of public affairs. We Socialists feel that they are a law unto themselves and whenever they do open their mouths 'let no dog bark'. But rest assured, whenever we find any of these gentlemen only half awake and likely to stumble, we shall be prepared to give them a friendly whack on the back in the shape of letters and protests. Whether the Town Clerk enters them on the agenda paper or not is a matter of indifference to us.

We shall continue to prod the occupants of our Corporation menagerie and look on and enjoy the fun of the best show in Hastings. Our friend Councillor March by the way only just missed being the originator of the Hastings branch of the S.D.F. At the last meeting of the now defunct local N.D.L he moved that they should become a branch of the Social Democratic Federation: that proposition was not taken up then. The Socialists started their own organisation later without asking Mr March's permission, henceforth his displeasure. (But we will kindly set the guileless Willie right in his remarks.) The local branch of the S.D.F have had the same secretary from the commencement of its existence to the present time, not three in three months. I must flatly contradict his statement that any Social Democrat took part in the begging parades in our streets recently, as that is utterly against our principles. We believe in justice not charity. It is the duty of a well-organised community to find useful employment for all its members and to see that none of them go short of their requirements of life. We plead guilty to being coffee house politicians, we believe in paying for a room off licensed premises in preference to meeting at a place which we could have for the mere wet rent.

But never mind Willie, the time is fast approaching when we shall again occupy our open air meeting place at the Fishmarket forum.

Then the March winds may bluster and blow at those wicked Socialists who will persistently, in and out of season, point out the iniquities of the present system of government and voice the wrongs of the masses of the people against the classes who are content to say 'God's in his heaven: all's well'.[7]

Not content with urging the Town Council to enforce the halfpenny rate, James Kerr wrote a few days later to the Distress Committee. Distress

Committees were appointed under the Unemployed Workman's Act of 1905. They were funded by charitable subscription with local Councils providing the Committee's expenses. Kerr set forth a S.D.F. scheme for transforming the Pilot Field ground into a number of allotments. He estimated the scheme would keep 50 people employed for three months making the sports ground a far better source of revenue to the town. The Distress Committee did not exactly approve of the idea of breaking up the field 'for agricultural or gardening purposes' but replied to Kerr indicating any decision must rest with the local Board of Guardians. The idea was not taken up.

Alf Cobb was well aware of the pathetic inadequacy of charitable donations. These subscriptions were the only safety net for the town's growing numbers of unemployed. Early in March 1907 he pressed the Hastings authorities to act to relieve the desperate plight of the unemployed:

> I attended the Town Council meeting upon Friday last, as I was interested to know what our Town Councillors were prepared to do for our unemployed, knowing as I did that a resolution was submitted from the Social Democratic Federation calling their attention to the large number of out-of-works, and to the insufficient amount of the cash in hand held by the Distress Committee to effectively cope with the distress prevailing.
>
> In order to prove the truth of the latter statement I would take the month of January. During that period 620 men applied for the application forms, on the other hand £340 was subscribed. If the whole sum was expended in wages by the Distress Committee, it would still require a few more pounds to allow each of the 620 men who are out of work the remuneration of five pence per day.
>
> These facts prove conclusively what the Social Democrats have endeavoured to impress upon the Town Council from the first, viz., that the sum of money obtained by the Distress Committee is totally inadequate to satisfactorily meet the requirements, and again the Town Council should move in the matter, not leaving entirely to charity. Up to now something like 730 men have applied for the necessary forms, this by the way does not by any means represent the whole number out of work, the 270 required to make the total 1000 could, I believe, be easily found.
>
> We Socialists believe that where unemployment exists, through no fault of the person unemployed, it is the duty of the town authority to at once deal with the question and find temporary work of a useful kind. At the last Council meeting

both Aldermen and Councillors who favoured the displacement of granite on our roads by bluestone, waxed eloquent as to how this would mean labour for our out-of works, but whilst devoting their eloquence to a mere side issue, were very silent about our resolution which offered them every opportunity of discussing the question in its broad aspects.

The fact is they do not care a snap of their fingers for our unemployed townsmen, the pity of it is, that November is ten long weary months ahead, but the doings of some of these Town Councillors will not be forgotten and in December next some of them, as far as our town affairs are concerned, will themselves be compelled to join the ranks of the unemployed.[8]

The 'great social evil' of unemployment had been Tom Kennedy's major theme in a series of public addresses given from his Clarion Van – a horse drawn speaker's platform. One of the National Democratic League's last initiatives was to engage Kennedy for a week's political campaign in Hastings. In the week commencing November 18th, 1906 he held nightly meetings at the Fishmarket or by the Yacht Stade at Harold Place, apart from his Wednesday evening address in the Public Hall.

Tom Kennedy was a well-known Northern orator. He had charge of one of three Clarion vans engaged in a countrywide tour to spread the cause of Socialism. Hastings was the first town in Sussex Kennedy had touched. The local press hailed him as 'a star in the socialist midst' although he spoke entirely under the auspices of the N.D.L.

The *Clarion* weekly newspaper had been published under the guiding hand of Robert Blatchford, regularly since December 1891. As a journalist, Blatchford had a rare talent. He could convey the Socialist message in an ardent and popular style. A series of his articles, inviting John Smith (a typical working man) to join the Socialist ranks was extracted from the Clarion and published in the book *Merrie England*. George Meek, the S.D.F.'s first guest speaker had formed the Eastbourne Clarion Fellowship, which sold both Blatchford's *Clarion* weekly and his reprinted work *Merrie England*.

Young Tom Kennedy was well chosen as a Clarion 'Vanner'. Local reporters stressed his remarkable talent as a platform speaker. They confessed to have heard few men equally able to express themselves so clearly and intelligently. They did not doubt that he had left an indelible impression upon the minds of the crowds he addressed. On the Tuesday evening Kennedy spoke brilliantly on the Education question from a workman's standpoint openly admitting that socialists were advocating a revolutionary policy. He had been shown a report of the meeting of the Hastings Education Committee and thought that a more undemocratic method of administering to the mental needs of the children could not be pursued.

He was received with wild enthusiasm at an indoor meeting at the Market Hall. Members of the N.D.L. and the S.D.F. were in good attendance. He chose the subject of his address 'The Relation of Labour to Liberalism' in the mistaken assumption that Hastings was represented by a Liberal M.P. He corrected this impression by admitting 'I have been informed that Hastings has the misfortune to be represented by a Tory member.' Later he was to denounce the past record of the Liberal Party and its consistent opposition to working class interests.

Kennedy's mistake was understandable. Harvey du Cros, the Tory candidate, had sensationally defeated the Liberal, Freeman-Thomas, in a large poll at the 1906 General Election. His victory not only defied national trends but was a complete reversal of the political tide then sweeping the country. His opponent's defeat was regarded as the greatest surprise ever known in the Borough. The Liberal *Weekly Mail and Times* was unable to suppress its displeasure and:

> ...disgust at the ludicrous position in which our town is placed in view of the overwhelming opinion of the country against Mr Balfour, Mr Chamberlain and all their works... twelve months ago when we were told by an eminent supporter of the Conservative cause in Hastings that the town would stand by the man with the most money, we refused to believe it. Du Cros came and aided by powerful combinations, strange artifice, peculiar methods, his capital triumphed.

Tressell and a Liberal newspaper had reached the same conclusion: Mugsborough was a rotten borough!

By April 1907, Hastings Social Democrats were holding branch meetings every Thursday evening at the Pelham Dining Rooms, 5 Pelham Street. A. C. Wingfield was listed in *Justice* as General Secretary. Edward Cruttenden (who would cycle to Eastbourne to meet his friend George Meek) forwarded the branch's third report to the London journal that month: 'With the help of our Tunbridge Wells comrades we have planted a healthy little branch of the S.D.F. in this old Cinque Port.'[9]

The self-congratulation was fully deserved.

CHAPTER 5

MUGSBOROUGH'S TWO SOCIALIST CAMPS

As the dreary winter months of 1906/7 passed, Frank Willard grudgingly accepted that politically he was still out in the cold. He had resigned his membership of the S.D.F. in January 1907 under humiliating circumstances. Shortly after his departure a small group of his closest admirers followed his lead. Willard and his loyal band of supporters made plans to set up a rival Socialist organisation. The formation of a local independent Labour Party branch would effectively cut short the political isolation of Willard's admirers and split Mugsborough's socialists into two competing camps. Social Democrats were convinced that Willard established a branch of the I.L.P. in Hastings out of sheer spite against his former colleagues. Virtually compelled to resign, he had suffered an acute loss of face. This was his means of retaliation.

Whilst the intrigue and speculation continued, a public meeting was fixed for the evening of April 16th, 1907 to discuss the prospects of forming an I.L.P. branch. It was chaired by Walter Campling, Secretary of the Trades and Labour Council, at Ferrari's Restaurant in Havelock Road. Many of the best-known local socialists were present, including Alf Cobb and Edward Cruttenden. Willard was conspicuous in his absence, but the S.D.F. branch members who attended the meeting were well aware that he was behind the initiative although their knowledge that Willard was hell bent on attaining the leadership of the I.L.P. was not publicly disclosed. During the debate very few Social Democrats raised any objection to the move, apart from Cruttenden, who questioned whether there were sufficient local socialists to warrant another branch. He asked pointedly if there was anything preventing those present from joining the S.D.F. Councillor Reed agreed it was a mistake to have two socialist bodies in the town but hoped the S.D.F. might 'throw in its lot with the new I.L.P. branch.' It was left to Barclay Hanbury, a close associate of Willard's, to attempt to justify the meeting's purpose. He believed that, for a good many individuals, the Social Democrats went too far but thought the two bodies could fight side by side. Alf Cobb dismissed the idea that the S.D.F. was more extreme than the I.L.P.:

When the I.L.P. was first formed in 1893 my father and I
were among the first adherents; the only difference is that by
joining the I.L.P. people can escape being called Socialists.

After a long discussion covering the policy claims of the two societies, it was left to a leading Social Democrat, F. Owen, to move that an I.L.P. branch be formed. There had been no serious opposition from S.D.F. members in the audience although Cobb had drawn laughter and applause by informing the gathering it was not S.D.F. practice to form a branch in towns where an I.L.P. branch already existed. When an amendment was made to Owen's proposal by Councillor Reed that it was undesirable to have two distinct socialist parties in Hastings it received no support. Owen's resolution was carried.

As a Christian-Socialist, Frank Willard would have a greater affinity with the I.L.P. movement. The religious strain in British Socialism is normally ascribed to the Independent Labour Party, whereas the S.D.F. is far more noted for its Marxist secular radicalism.

In May 1907 the Hastings Trades Council received a communication from the Social Democrats asking if the branch could be affiliated. Walter Campling had tendered his resignation and the Council was now chaired by W. W. Jones. He spoke out forcefully against the 'Socialists' being admitted – if they had any sympathy with the true cause of labour they would be trade unionists. His remarks brought a sharp response from James Kerr in a written communiqué. It stated that the Chairman's knowledge of Socialists and their 'sympathy with trade unions must be very remote indeed.' Kerr insisted that his branch members were devoted trade unionists with a large percentage holding positions in trade union organisations, 'although not locally'. After Jones' remarks, the S.D.F. 'begged to withdraw its application for affiliation'.

Nationally, the S.D.F. had an old-fashioned attitude to trade unionism. The Federation had been formed when only a small minority of skilled workers belonged to craft unions. The national leadership believed that the unions, as allies of Liberalism, had constantly acted as a bulwark to capitalism and the struggle for improved wages and hours was politically inadequate. H. M. Hyndman, for instance, did not believe in strikes – strike pay would have been much better spent on socialist propaganda. And so W. W. Jones had a point.

The *Justice* issue of June 1st 1907 shows George Meek in a wildly optimistic mood concerning Hastings' future. He had been on a recent tour of South Eastern towns. In this passage Meek speaks of Edward Cruttenden as 'our dear comrade':

> For had we not kept the Red Flag, if not flying, at least in the very warmest of our hearts through long, dark and weary years? And had we not both, only a year ago, brought that same red flag once more out into the light of day to wave before the startled eyes of oppression and all its minions? There is a fire smouldering among those same hills of that ancient port which will some day help to illuminate the world, and burn away some, if not all, of its dross.

Cruttenden had attempted to establish a new socialist party in Hastings in 1895. In April that year he wrote to the *Hastings Observer* asking to 'hear from any friends of labour who will assist to set the progressive movement on its legs in the town – there is plenty of room for meetings on the beach.' It proved a false dawn for Socialism in Mugsborough.

Through the summer of 1907 there was scarcely a pause in the Socialist campaign with a series of outdoor addresses and debates. The I.L.P. branch played second fiddle to the S.D.F. in the campaign and thereafter always remained in its political shadow. Only occasionally did the Press make any reference to the Hastings Independent Labour Party, although extensive coverage was given to a mass meeting the branch promoted in November at the Market Hall. The Hall was hired with the object of urging the Corporation to take immediate action to reduce unemployment and help feed the vast numbers of hungry school children. The seating accommodation was filled to capacity; many local unemployed workmen stood in the rear. Frank Willard, Walter Campling and Barclay Hanbury were amongst the Labour representatives on the platform. The platform speakers savaged the Town Council. Willard made a fiery speech rousing the audience to a great pitch of excitement: The Hastings Corporation 'was as rotten a body as any town on the South Coast possessed.' A burst of applause greeted the Chairman's advice to those present not to return to the Council 'either the land jobber or the house agent.' Campling repeated old N.D.L. policy when he implored the unemployed to register with the Distress Committee 'even though many felt disinclined to fill in record papers', but unless the Committee could show the Local Government Board that a large number of unemployed existed, the chances of obtaining a grant from that authority were small. If this failed he was prepared to assist in organising a demonstration of the unemployed. A neutral observer might have found it difficult to detect any difference between the defunct League and the new 'socialist' branch.

By July 1907, Alf Cobb's compelling talent as a mob orator was unmistakable to his colleagues. His prickly and abrasive style was never dull. A large crowd had gathered on the last day of June to hear him engage in debate, and an I.L.P. meeting 'booked' for the Fishmarket was abandoned. The debating point, whether or not any Liberal Party measures had benefited the working class, was opposed by Cobb under constant interruption. Expletives and other verbal abuse greeted his Liberal opponent from Tottenham. After the political banter, Alf touched on several local issues. He told the gathering that if the Board of Guardians gave assistance to the unemployed, the recipients lost their right to vote. To avoid this the Guardians termed the financial aid 'medical relief'. 'And who wanted to make old inmates of Hastings Workhouse have margarine instead of butter?' he asked. 'The Liberals' shouted back the crowd faithfully. Alf agreed:

> The Liberals voted for it and the Tories rescinded it. I am not here to pat Tories on the back but Liberals on the Town Council, or in their dealings with workmen's wages, are just as much the enemies of the working class.

One of the commonest charges levelled against the S.D.F. and Socialists generally was that before their political programme could be implemented first they had to mould an intractable human nature. Harry Quelch repudiated this belief one evening in June at a Social Democrat assembly east of the Lifeboat House. Quelch was a leading figure in the Federation and at the time Editor of its journal *Justice*. In London during the late 1880's Quelch had helped organise and drill the unemployed. He told his onlookers that not only was human nature shaped by the environment but it was quite possible for Social Democrat reforms to be secured under the present political structure. This did not challenge basic S.D.F. policy. The Federation accepted a period of transition was necessary in which progressive reforms or 'stepping stones to a happier period for the workers' could be secured, even though they stopped short of outright socialism.

Earlier that afternoon Harry Quelch had given an address at the Yacht Stade, opposite the Queen's Hotel. He emphasised the need for the working class to organise itself into a party hostile to all other political parties:

England possessed the most astute governing class in the world, and from time to time the working people had been gulled by promises from both sides, always expecting some good from a government representing the interests of the master class. I don't believe there is anything to choose between a Liberal and a Tory or if there is a microscope would be required to discover it.

Edward Cruttenden was elated. During the week of Quelch's visit, five dozen copies of *Justice* were sold: 'while ten months ago a copy of *Justice* was not to be had in the town'.

By August 1907 the local Tory establishment was showing signs of panic. It was disturbed by the likely effects of the constant barrage of Socialist agitation and propaganda, which went mostly unchallenged. Sunday after Sunday the Social Democrats addressed crowds of people on the beach. The Tory press urged someone to come forward to contradict 'this insidious doctrine' before it took root in the minds of the public. The *Hastings Observer*'s issue of August 10th published the following letter from Charles Davenport:

> With reference to Mr Chubb's letter ... I am glad to be able to inform him that the Primrose League is taking a very strong attitude in opposition to Socialism and I shall be very pleased to receive any suggestion he or others may wish to make as to the best means of nipping the noxious and revolutionary weed in the bud...
>
> I would point out that the Primrose League by its loyal adherence to the three principles of Maintenance of Religion, Constitution and Empire and by its splendid organisation and strength by numbers is most admirably equipped in every way to oppose the unwholesome doctrines of Socialists.

Alf Cobb had inevitably also read Chubb's public assault on the 'Menace of Socialism'. His reply was both witty and devastatingly informative:

> Your correspondent is a humorist. Whether his humour was born or acquired I will leave your reader to guess. He states that he has previously had no opportunity of studying Socialist propaganda. Yet for years Mr Chubb's shop has been a kind of depot for Socialist Literature. If a Socialist wanted a copy of *Justice*, the 'Labour Leader', or the *Clarion* he was always sure of getting them from your correspondent.

To claim that he spoke strongly against Secular Sunday Schools, your casual reader would infer that Mr Chubb had occupied the Socialist Platform and smote them hip and thigh.

But no; Mr Chubb, to use his own words, had only stood with his mouth open wide; he did not even speak to the lecturer, but did, as he always does, stand on the fringe of the audience to interject remarks to his immediate hearers, but never sufficiently loud enough for those whom he attacks to hear, or for the lecturer to reply. We can only hope that he and his volunteers will pluck up their courage and ply our speaker with intelligent opposition.

But suppose Mr Chubb's volunteers suggest to him the unwisdom of his supplying the intelligent Hastings inhabitants with such 'pernicious' journals as those Socialist publications I have mentioned, and that he had better leave the sale of them to us Socialists, who are always well supplied with them, what then? Failing his inability to do this, his volunteers might infer that your correspondent's main idea is profit 'first', principle 'last'.

Failing Mr Chubb's courage to oppose our male speakers, I may inform him that we shall shortly have another lady, Miss Mabel Hope, who will be at Hastings to speak for us.'[10]

(The first female speaker to address the Hastings S.D.F. had been a Miss Kathleen Kough, from London. She spoke at two meetings at the end of July 1907)

Chubb thanked Charles Davenport for his press announcement – he'd be at his service whenever convenient. His answer to Cobb's letter stretched the readers' imagination:

> What has my business got to do with my letters? I supply my customers' wants and honestly say that although I knew the *Clarion* to be Mr Blatchford's mouthpiece and he was an agnostic, I thought it was a Labour paper. 'The Labour Leader' I fancied was to tell labourers where work was to be had and *Justice* I imagined was a paper devoted to police reports, etc., until I was enlightened on the matter.

Chubb compounded his stupidity by sending the following extract from *Justice* on the spread of Socialism in Hastings to a local newspaper:

> The past two Sunday evenings have attracted immense crowds as to give the old capitalist parties shocks. The Tories look solemn and give ominous warnings and the Liberals want to bolster up a case of disorderly meetings. Both of the

political organs have struck up the same tune 'The Menace of Socialism' which they find has caught on here. The call for united action against us is responded to by half-pay officials, who want volunteers to make a united stand for class privileges and to make a determined onslaught on the forces of Socialism and disruption. But, despite the gallant Major (Davenport) and his host of Amazonian warriors of the Primrose League we'll keep the Red Flag flying here.[11]

Alf Cobb never let a chance go begging. He seized on Chubb's improbable statements in a sardonic retort published two weeks later:

Sir,
By your last issue I notice Mr Chubb has taken to reading *Justice* at last. Or was he merely looking for Police Court reports when his eye happened on our local notes?[12]

In the same copy of the newspaper a letter was published from Cobb to the Editor:

There is much joy in the Socialist Camp to know from the columns of your last issue that we are within reach of some intelligent opposition.

With your correspondent Major C. T. Davenport, we believe the Primrose League is admirably organised to uphold the principles of Empire and Constitution. We on our side welcome the news that they are equipped to combat what they choose to term the unwholesome doctrines of Socialists.

The S.D.F. branch then wrote to Davenport suggesting that the best means to oppose unwholesome doctrines was by public debate:

You on your side could appoint a worthy champion, also choose place of meeting and appoint the chairman. We on our side will provide someone to uphold the banner of Socialism.

The repeated 'we on our side' suggests Cobb penned the letter and the 'someone' was himself. The branch had total confidence in his powers of oratory and debating skill. It regularly encouraged its political opponents to engage in public debate. The challenge was rarely heeded and most often quietly ignored. When Tom Kennedy was last in Hastings the S.D.F. invited the 'Borough Member' Arthur du Cros to hold an open-air debate on Socialism. By early August the offer still had not been accepted, but remained open. Before the month of August was out, the Primrose League had also turned down the challenge of public debate. The branch received a letter from Major Davenport declining the invitation.

Cobb forwarded the letter to the local Press with an accompanying note:

> We are sorry Major Davenport does not see his way clear to arrange a series of debates, whereby the case for and against Socialism could be put in a clear and intelligent manner...[13]

Davenport had justified his refusal by saying that the proposed open-air debate did not meet the requirements of the case: from his observations no good result had ever been attained by these heated platform contests.

The refusal of du Cros or the Primrose League to be drawn into open public debate demonstrated an anxiety not to be outmanoeuvred or humiliated by Cobb's oratory flair and a fear that any such confrontation would only further encourage an already intensive S.D.F. propaganda campaign.

The Social Democrats also played a prominent part in the discussions at the Hastings Debating Society throughout the 1906 session. Their members dominated the proceedings, using every opportunity to be heard, often to the exclusion of other parties. But the Socialists were poorly represented on the Committee. Before the 1907 session started the Society contrived to rearrange the day of the meeting knowing that if it was held on a Thursday evening it would coincide with the weekly S.D.F. gathering at Pelham Dining Rooms. The move effectively excluded their attendance. The local Tory Press was jubilant: 'The Socialists are already booked for that evening; rumour hath it that the promoters of the Debating Society are not very despondent on this account.'[14]

In the second week of October 1907 Tom Kennedy returned to Hastings. He parked his *Clarion* van platform at street corners all over town. A news reporter noted that the week's propaganda had not been restricted to the east end of town. The Party with its red banner was conspicuous in central Hastings, at Silverhill and even so close to aristocratic circles as Pevensey Road, St. Leonards. At one evening meeting Kennedy pitched his *Clarion* platform at the side of Silverlands Road and spoke way after the legally permitted time. His voice was only once drowned out when a Salvation Army band passed slowly by. The following evening he bitterly condemned the Hastings Corporation for caring more about 'beautifying' the local Parks and Gardens than the 'cultivation of child life and a healthy citizenship'. Kennedy's week-long visit was so successful that the S.D.F. retained his services for an additional seven days. At South Terrace, in mid-

October, he scornfully dismissed the political arguments of the town's Tory MP: 'du Cros's reasoning is so trivial and has been replied to so many times from our platform, it is like flogging a dead horse to attempt to criticise it'. Before du Cros again spoke in public he should attempt to understand the principles of Socialism: 'He would then save himself from a position in which he now stands, a position in which he is the object of ridicule and contempt of every individual in Hastings who understands Socialism.'

That summer of 1907 the Tunbridge Wells Socialist Sunday School had visited Hastings. The Tory Hastings Advertiser expressed apparent horror on reading the School's 'Red Catechism' containing its secular creed:

> In this booklet the working classes are represented in the
> depths of poverty and misery while every employer of labour
> is a bigoted, merciless monster, whose only desire is to suck
> the blood of the working man who is robbed and tossed
> from the frying pan into the fire and back again...[15]

Local newspapers questioned why there was such a persistent Socialist campaign in a seaside resort where the industrial population was tiny. The impression of one Liberal weekly editorial was that the S.D.F. calculated on making easy converts amongst the large body of needy people in the Borough, 'many of whom have only too much time to dwell upon the illusory roads to better conditions'. [16]

By the autumn, a section of the Press were actively encouraging the shelving of the policy of quietly ignoring the flood tide of Socialism hoping it would eventually subside:

> It is of course wrong to suppose that all the working men of
> Hastings are Socialists already, but it will not be the fault of
> agitators if the majority are not at least in sympathy with
> them before they are finished. *They must be opposed* – met on
> their own ground by capable and able speakers who can hold
> their own with the glib tongued orators who expound the
> Socialistic doctrines in such a captivating manner. For people
> of the ordinary calibre to go to the meetings and ask
> questions is only to give the speakers an opportunity of
> crushing them and thereby showing their audience how
> apparently indisputable are their statements. [17]

The last public meeting on the S.D.F. 1907 calendar occurred in the second week of December. The Brighton socialist orator, William Evans, implored the Hastings workless to make themselves an unmitigated nuisance to the authorities until something was done. He had been told the Council disapproved of the street parades. His rhetorical question 'Did the Councillors prefer the unemployed to stay at home and die like rats in a hole' was interpreted as incitement. The local tabloids reacted hysterically, calling his address inflammatory by urging the unemployed to violence. Evans was dismayed at the begging parades he had witnessed: 'It is a contemptible spectacle to see the British working man either full of beer and 'baccy' singing 'Rule Britannia' when he was in work or marching round the streets singing 'We've got no work to do'. Far better to send a deputation of unemployed visiting Councillors' homes especially if they resided the more fashionable quarters. Why wasn't the Church helping them by putting 'the doctrine of the Man of Nazareth into practice?'

Alf Cobb had chaired the platform. He took up Evans' theme. He'd noticed that the Distress Committee Fund stood at a paltry £100 while the Churches had raised £2000 by holding several bazaars the week before: 'it seems to show that they care more about people's souls than their bodies.' This was a recurring Socialist theme. Cobb advocated:

> That the various organisations in the town – Socialist, Trade and Friendly Societies – organise a monster procession on Christmas Day without 'collection boxes', appealing for 'work' not 'charity' for the purpose of bringing to the notice of the local authorities and our wealthier citizens the amount of poverty and suffering existing in the town. I feel sure that if this is done, headed by a representative of each organisation, our silent out-of-work sufferers would turn out in their hundreds, as the present processions in. no way represent the amount of distress which prevails.

CHAPTER 6

THE REACTIONARY BACKLASH

Early in 1908 the local Social Democrats took the obvious move and switched their weekly evening meetings at the Pelham Dining Rooms to another weekday, so avoiding the engineered clash with the Debating Society. The first half of the year saw a rapid interchange of branch secretary: Wingfield relinquished the post to Cecil Powe; Powe was displaced by Edward Cruttenden and Albert Sellens, a close friend of Robert Tressell, replaced Cruttenden two months later. Finally the branch membership appointed Alf Cobb to the leadership of the Hastings S.D.F. in July 1908. It was belated official recognition of a talent that eclipsed all others in the movement and a tribute to his inspirational energy and political commitment. After Cobb took over as branch secretary there was only one minor change before the outbreak of war led to the branch's inevitable break up. In 1912 Alf switched from secretary to treasurer to defend the branch funds against a claim for libel damages.

During Cruttenden's short tenure as Secretary, he had been impressed by the many occasions visitors had asked him to explain the reason for there being so many unemployed 'loafing around our thoroughfares and such hordes of unkempt, hungry looking children infesting the streets; the questioners hardly expect such conditions to prevail in a fashionable seaside resort'.

Although the Provision of Meals Act allowed local authorities to combat the numbers of underfed schoolchildren by raising an additional rate, Mugsborough's officialdom showed a marked reluctance to take this step. In December 1906 the Chairman of the Education Committee publicly declared that he was satisfied the stage had not yet been reached to adopt the Act in Hastings. His judgement showed either an abysmal ignorance or wicked complacency. The Education Committee even doubted the evidence and reports received from their own head teachers. But their hands were forced in January 1908 – charitable funds and subscriptions were at their lowest level for two years and the numbers of unemployed registered with the Distress Committee had risen inexorably. The Council finally ratified a proposal to spend £100 out of the rates to cover the provision of food at sixteen local schools. The sustained

J.W.E. CHUBB

John. W.E. Chubb
St Nicolas Church
HASTINGS

Alf Cobb's most fervent adversary, John William Evan Chubb, was one of the great 'characters' of the Old Town. As well as sparring with each other in the correspondence column of the local newspaper, Chubb and Alf Cobb had several verbal run-ins, and Chubb once angrily tore down the Social Democratic Party flag during a beach meeting.

Born in 1856, young John grew up in Wellingborough, where he was successively a choirboy, organ scholar, sub-vicar, organist and choirmaster. His Temperance Choir won an award. He married Mary Ann Cleavely in 1877 and had three daughters.

Although his life was devoted to the church, to make a living he ran a newsagent's shop. His wife's illness in 1884 prompted the family to move to Hastings, then famous for its curative sea air. After a brief sojourn at 100 Bohemia Road they took over a newsagent at 59 George Street and lived above the shop, where Mrs. Chubb bore a son.

The whole family soon became deeply involved with various activities at St Clement's Church, where Chubb was a sidesman. He had a fine tenor voice and joined the church choirs of St Clement's, St Paul's (now demolished), St John's and St Mary-in-the-Castle.

Chubb arranged many meetings and entertainments for workers (especially fishermen) at the Fisherman's Institute and ran an eisteddfod in the Market Hall. At the relief of Mafeking (Boer War) he organised a great outdoor thanksgiving meeting. Chubb was a fervent advocate of temperance and founded the All Saints' and St Clement's Temperance Society. Of course, none of his family was allowed intoxicating liquor.

Although not a brilliant musical performer, Chubb was passionate about music. He assisted the organist at St Mary and wrote some hymn tunes. His children were all taught to play the organ. Two of his daughters became church organists and his son was an organ scholar at St John's. In 1900 he started collecting money for an organ for the Chapel of St Nicholas (more commonly known as the Fishermen's Church, and now a museum); however, he only raised enough for a harmonium. (He always believed it deserved a proper pipe-organ and, in his seventies, resurrected the organ fund).

When the curate left in 1918, Chubb took over the Chapel and became lay reader-in-charge, having been licensed by the Bishop of Lewes. (He had known the Bishop years before, when he was the Reverend T. W. Cook of Wellingborough, and later when he was the Rector of Holy Trinity, Hastings).

Chubb was totally devoted to the Fishermen's Church. It was his life's work, and he did everything he could to make the church an active mission and an influence for good. As well as playing the organ, he arranged the daily services, trained a choir, founded a Boys' Club and a Sisterhood, and established a Rogationtide ritual: The Blessing of the Sea. He made great improvements to the building, adding a vestry and a prayer chapel, and had the east end rebuilt. Because of his many activities, Chubb became a very prominent character in the Old Town and before long everyone was calling him 'Father Chubb'.

As Vice-President of the Conservative Club, Father Chubb served on several committees, made public speeches, and organised a Conservative working men's meeting in the Old Town. Although he stood for election (unsuccessfully) to the School Board and the Board of Guardians, he declined to seek election to the Town Council.

After retiring as a newsagent, Father Chubb moved to a house named 'St Nicholas', at 34 Athelstan Road, opposite All Soul's Church. He died of throat cancer in 1929. A long obituary appeared in the *Hastings & St Leonards Observer*, and a lengthy report of his funeral appears the following week, together with a photograph. Present at the funeral was Lord Eustace Percy, who was an old friend of Father Chubb, and a great number of clergymen, four of whom conducted the service.

Father Chubb's son, like Alf Cobb's daughter, emigrated to Canada in the 1920s. Father Chubb's daughter Edith is featured in my *Notable Women of Victorian Hastings*, Hastings Press, 2002.

HELENA WOJTCZAK

opposition of public officials and Councillors to any legislation regarded as vaguely socialistic was one reason why Hastings was so backward in applying the Act.

A month after the additional rate was first imposed a working class audience packed the Market Hall to hear a discussion on the twin causes of the workless worker and the hungry child. This meeting immediately followed a communication from Cobb to the Education Committee suggesting the present members made way for others. Alf was at the Market Hall that February night. He moved a resolution protesting against the modest deployment of 'our local bodies' administrative powers and contemptuously ridiculed the feeding of skimmed milk to hungry schoolchildren. The people of Hastings would not object, if they realised there were more than 350 children starving in the town, to paying a halfpenny rate to have them fed. Guest speaker for the evening was R C. Morrison, a London Social Democrat. Before leaving the City a friend had placed in his hands a booklet advertising the charms of Hastings. To Morrison, it seemed strange that Hastings should be advertised as a health resort when there were several hundred of the town's children underfed. He read a letter from the Town Clerk to the Education Committee inviting tenders for skimmed milk to be supplied for schoolchildren's breakfasts. Was it good enough for their children to be fed skimmed milk after parents had toiled their hardest to keep the wolf from the door, he asked. Why, there's not a single Hastings Councillor who would feed his poodle on skimmed milk. He wished he had been present at the very first school breakfasts – then he could have told members of the Education Committee the story of the farmer who had put his cow to graze on top of the mountain where there was very little fodder. The cow grew thinner and thinner. The farmer said to the cow, named Maggie: 'Maggie, I'm very sorry you have not got much to eat, but you have a very fine, view.' When the audience's laughter subsided, Morrison referred to 'that saving clause the little children of Hastings possess which the London children have not got – a fine view.'

During that winter of 1907/8 the special powers under the Provision of Meals Act were employed to a minimal extent and hastily dropped once the season was officially judged over. The supply of skimmed milk to be used with the children's breakfast of porridge, bread, butter and sugar was continued – no meat dinner was provided. Alf Cobb researched the full provisions of the Act and made them available to the public:

The Act states that if the children are attending our schools without sufficient food that the Education Committee may (not that it shall) undertake the feeding of those children: money can be expended locally in this direction to about £800. It does not limit the number of meals. It does not limit the number of days on which they may be fed. Thus, if three meals per day were considered necessary by the local authority, there is no one to say nay. If, again, the local authority discovers that the children, during school holidays, are being insufficiently fed, they may, without hindrance from the Board of Education, arrange for meals to be supplied.'[18]

Edward Cruttenden bitterly condemned the scheme's implementation as hesitant and parsimonious and attacked the sly manner in which it was abandoned without any report being made. Socialist agitation must continue, he said, until the feeding of schoolchildren was made compulsory.

By July 1908 local reports suggest that the Socialists were taking Mugsborough by storm. Meetings were held on an ambitious scale. One in particular was extensively covered by the Press. The drama unfolded on a Friday evening at the junction of South Terrace and Queen's Road. A section of the published article captures well the flavour of the gathering:

The Socialists had pitched their banner and their platform, both of the same gory red colour on the patch of stone just by a water hydrant, as they had done many times before and Mr Cobb having delivered a preliminary speech as Chairman, the London orator, Mr Ernest Hunter, started upon a fiery discourse, which consisted of the usual violent denunciations of both political parties, a fierce denial of the charges of Atheism and immorality brought against the Socialists and sweeping condemnation of the landlord, the capitalist and the rentlord, which he described as an 'unholy trinity of interests.'

As usual, a goodly sized crowd, consisting of curious idlers, youths smoking cigarettes, and old women wondering what it was about, gradually gathered around, bringing in its train three policemen, a sergeant and two constables. They stood on the outskirts of the crowd for a while and then consulted with Mr Cobb, one of them produced a notebook.

Shortly afterwards, right in the middle of his oration, the speaker got down from the platform and gave way to Mr Cobb, who appealed to the crowd to close up and keep the pavement clear, as the police were watching them that evening and were intent on making a case against them. Following this appeal, he entered into a tirade against the local authorities who, he said, were behind the police, making them harry the Socialists, because they were afraid of their growing strength in the town. The police, he said, had to please their good friends, the Councillors, so while they prosecuted hawkers, and Socialists, they did not interfere with Councillors who offended the bylaws.

Remounting the platform the orator observed that Hastings was not a working class constituency, said that the population consisted of merry widows and miserable or languid Johnnies. Eventually when the speaker declared that under the present system of society, the motto was: 'Do others or they will do you', a man called out three times: 'That's it', and then crying: 'Good night' departed waving a pipe in the air. Hunter called after him: 'Goodnight, and don't come back too soon' and resumed his speech.

Cobb made a few more remarks about the police. Of course, he realised that they had to obey their Liberal and Conservative masters and he hoped that the time would come, as come it would one day in the lifetime of the Constables present there, when the Socialists would be in the majority on the Council. Then he would like to see the faces of those policemen when they had to touch their caps to a Socialist Councillor.

The crowd having laughed merrily at this sally, Mr Cobb went on to talk about the police attack on the hawker, and the measures which those people were taking to defend themselves. Contrasting that with the present attack on himself that evening, he said that if he were summoned and convicted for obstruction he would not pay a fine. No, what he would do would be to make the ratepayers keep him in Lewes Gaol.

When Cobb had finished answering questions, the constables devoted their attention to him and took his name and address in the presence of a large and curious crowd. Which done, Mr Cobb declared the meeting closed and the little band of Socialists showed their defiance of the police by closing round and singing their evening hymn.'[19]

Alf Cobb invested many hours studiously boning up on the local bylaws until he knew them backwards. He drew on this wide knowledge to defend himself against trumped up charges of bylaw infringement and as a means of counterattack to underline the selective use of the legislation by the town's authorities. His endeavours to clear the onlookers obstructing the pavement would, he knew, provide a legitimate defence in court. His observations on the police showed a typical bravado.

As Cobb anticipated, both he and Hunter were later summoned for obstructing the highway. Hunter's case was adjourned since he had another summons to answer elsewhere on the same day. Alf pleaded not guilty. He conducted his own case seated at the solicitor's table in the Police Court. On the desk was a batch of papers, which he frequently consulted. He called a Dairyman S.D.F. 'comrade' for the defence. The witness vigorously denied that Cobb had placed the speaker's platform in the road – it was there before the meeting started. No, he could not account for how the platform came to be brought to South Terrace: 'It was usually kept at the coffee room where the comrades meet, but it may have been kept at Middle Street where Mr Cobb lives'. When the police admitted that the defendant had requested the crowd to keep clear of the pavement Cobb glared at the Magistrate and asked: 'Then how can I have wilfully obstructed the highway?' The Magistrate had little option in fining him a small sum for a purely technical offence.

The object of the sudden rigid observance of bylaws covering highway obstruction was to intimidate leading Socialist agitators and stifle the spread of their doctrine. That summer the Corporation extended the same laws to barrow and basket trading in the town's central thoroughfares. The unprecedented crackdown on street hawkers was the direct consequence of an orchestrated protest by tradesmen who occupied highly rated business premises in prominent shopping areas.

Acting under instructions, the Chief Constable encouraged the vigorous enforcement of regulations designed to free the public highway from inconvenience to traffic. Hawkers were warned off stretches of the beach unless they had recognised stall sites. Roadways near the town centre were heavily patrolled by police. On a single day in July, twenty hawkers were brought before the Borough Bench. Included among those charged with obstruction was Elizabeth Todd who had sold shrimps and prawns from her basket at Harold Place. Six weeks later Mrs. Todd was again hauled before the Magistrates to answer charges of obstructing the roadway with two large shrimp baskets. She complained bitterly in Court that she had been selling shrimps in Harold Place unmolested for twenty-three years. The anti-obstruction regulations were carried out with such thoroughness that even two small boys were charged with selling postcards on the beach. These harsh and draconian measures led Alf Cobb to make a public appeal to local residents:

> The Hastings hawkers earnestly appeal to you to enter your protest against the harsh treatment which is being meted to them by the police, who – acting under orders of the Watch Committee, who in turn are bowing to the agitation of a few unreasonable shopkeepers – are reporting and issuing summonses for the most trivial reasons.

Hawkers, without doubt, supply a much-needed want, both to the poorer class of visitors and residents, and they feel that reasonable use of the highway should be allowed them for display of their wares and to serve customers.

Under the Highway Act, the mere staying the progress of a barrow, the placing of a basket upon the ground to serve a customer, is – in the eyes of a Bench of Magistrates, who have already had pressure brought to bear upon them by the shopkeepers mentioned – an offence, punishable by fine, with alternative of imprisonment.

If hawking is restricted, your fruit, fish and other foodstuffs will cost you more.

Meetings will be held every evening, commencing Monday, July 13th, at 7.30 p.m. in Queen's Road, opposite Cricketer's Hotel. All in sympathy with a struggling class of your fellow townsmen are invited to attend.

Signed, on behalf of the hawkers,

Alfred Cobb.

A circular that he helped print addressed to the 'citizens of Hastings and all lovers of justice' rapidly flooded the streets. One paragraph asked if the people were aware a great crime was being committed in their midst. Another read:

Your servile police authorities, owing to the action of a few greedy, unscrupulous, grasping, unchristian shopkeepers who do not care who starves as long as they live, have started a campaign of persecution against a section of traders called hawkers, who fulfil a public service.

The *Hastings Observer* thought that the Magistrates had been too lenient with offending hawkers: 'Because tradesmen seek to protect themselves against unlawful and unfair competition they are all that is vile in the eyes of the agitators and of alien street vendors.' The paper believed the hawkers were both unwise and foolish 'in listening to the voice of that agitator Cobb who eggs them on to break the law'. Street traders disregarded such advice. That summer of 1908 Alf Cobb adopted a new role as hawker's champion.

The first evening rally in support of the hawkers was the most eventful. Alf mounted a rostrum at the corner of South Terrace. He spoke for nearly an hour with several other hawkers in close attention. He announced that street collections for a defence fund had already started. Three policemen listened attentively to his remarks, watching the proceedings almost

BOOKS

Women of Victorian Sussex
Their Status, Occupations & Dealings with the Law
by Helena Wojtczak
£9.99 (postage £2)

Railwaywomen
Exploitation, Betrayal and Triumph in the Workplace
by Helena Wojtczak
Hardback 384 pages. £20 (postage £5.00)

 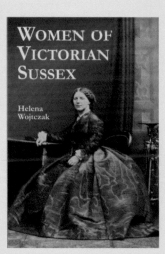

Poor Cottages and Proud Palaces
The Life and Work of Thomas Sockett of Petworth 1777-1859
by Sheila Haines and Leigh Lawson
£9.99 (postage £1.20) (Pub. late 2007)

Footplate to Footpath
The Lost Railways of the Isle of Wight
by Adrian Hancock
£12 (postage £2) (pub. Autumn 2007)

Notable Women of Victorian Sussex
A Collection of Mini-Biographies
by Val Brown & Helena Wojtczak
£9.99 (postage £2) (pub. late 2007)

Alf Cobb: Mugsborough Rebel
The Struggle for Justice in Edwardian Hastings
by Mike Matthews
£6.99 (postage £1.20)

Captain Swing in Sussex and Kent
Rural Rebellion in 1830
by Mike Matthews
£7.99 (postage £1.20)

Women's Hospitals in Brighton & Hove
The Lady Chichester & New Sussex Hospitals
by Val Brown
£7.50 (postage £1.20)

Matilda Betham-Edwards
Novelist, Travel Writer and Francophile
by Joan Rees
£9.99 (postage £1.20)

throughout. He explained it was the jealousy of a few tradesmen who had influence on the Council that had prompted the severe restrictions and numerous prosecutions:

> The Hastings Authorities have very peculiar views of what constituted an obstruction. The Chief Constable's definition was very harsh towards men who earnestly desire to earn an honest living in a manner they had chosen. It's quite evident that last year's bylaws passed against beach hawking were passed by people who are in some way biased against hawkers.
>
> Since these biased individuals were the very magistrates that sat in judgement at the Police Court, the case against a hawker was practically decided in advance.

He advocated, that evening, the right to live without application for relief to the Distress Committee or the Guardians.

Cobb's energy was unflagging – his commitment to a cause total. He had an immense capacity for hard work. Already his resistance to the new measures taken by the Hastings authorities to drive the hawkers off the streets included a public appeal, distribution of leaflets, a week of platform speaking and the establishment of a defence fund. Hawkers watched in admiration as this self-educated and gifted individual slaved away relentlessly on their behalf. Once the evening meetings were complete, Alf moved the battle onto a different front. He publicly announced the names of the two leading figures behind the prosecutions as Mr Apel and Councillor Cox:

> It seems to me most peculiar that the hawkers were continually moved on by a policeman, with their barrows, while you can find the latter gentleman's breadtrucks in the streets outside his shop morning after morning. One morning I went into the shop to buy a penny bun. I asked the girl behind the counter whether they didn't get into trouble for leaving the truck there. 'Oh no,' she replied. 'It stands there all day if we don't want it.'

He informed the shop assistant that she could tell Councillor Cox 'since he was so down on the hawkers' that he was going to take out a summons against him for allowing the truck to remain so long in the roadway.

He then directed his attention to Mr Apel. There was a bylaw stating that all newspaper boards placed outside shops must not project into the road, yet Apel had his placards stuck out on the public highway. He and a companion had once measured them – they protruded over eighteen inches into the pathway. The 'eagle-eyed' policeman on point duty did not apprehend coachmen and footmen waiting with their carriages in Robertson Street outside business establishments. Alf vastly entertained his sympathetic audience by relating what had recently happened outside the General Post Office when a 'certain motor car drew up'. The policeman on duty at the Memorial engaged in humorous conversation with the driver and after the gentleman returned from the Post Office and entered his car, the policeman touched his hat. 'They don't do that to hawkers' he added, to hearty laughter.

The friendly atmosphere altered dramatically when a character called Jack Buss elbowed his way to the front of the crowd to engage Alf in a heated argument. Polly Bassett was amongst the spectators, flushed and furious, she seized hold of Buss's jacket stopping his progress to the platform. Clearly outraged, she shook him angrily and struck him in the face with her clenched fist. Alf hurriedly concluded his speech with another appeal for public support. Two days later he publicly challenged Councillor Cox to contest the 'hawking question' either on an indoor or outdoor platform.

Cobb kept his word to Cox's shop assistant and applied for a summons against Atkins Bros and Cox for obstructing the highway with their vehicle. He was informed by the Chairman of the Magistrates that he must meet the prosecution costs; 'I can't afford to pay,' answered Alf, 'but I had hoped the Magistrates would treat the case without prejudice.' After he was threatened for contempt of Court Alderman Langham insisted: 'We are never prejudiced – you can have the summons in the ordinary way if you can afford it.'

Jack Buss, however, was not so restricted financially. He summoned Polly for assault. Buss was described in Court as a carman, residing in Priory Street. He said, in evidence, that after leaving the Cricketer's he noticed Cobb addressing a mob: 'I told him he didn't know what he was talking about – we want different men to lead our cause. Suddenly this lady rushed through and hit me on the side of the head, a regular stinger; then instantly she clawed hold of my whiskers and shook me.'

Polly Bassett, in defence, became heated and indignant. She cross-questioned Buss with such blazing fury she had to be restored to order. Buss, she cried, came upon a meeting in a drunken condition – he struck her on the breast and she retaliated by 'catching hold of his whiskers'. Alf spoke in her defence – the complainant had interrupted an orderly meeting.

When Buss craftily asked Cobb's relationship to the defendant, Polly rose from her seat and boldly replied: 'he is my young man'. She was fined 5s with 18s costs.

'I won't pay a penny,' exclaimed Polly.

'Then seven days', replied the Chairman. Polly paid up.

Two weeks after Polly Bassett's conviction for assault J. Chubb, the shopkeeper who thought his copies of *Justice* contained police reports, once again tried to disrupt a Sunday evening Social Democratic address at the Fishmarket. He endeavoured to haul down the red S.D.P. flag to the intense displeasure of the branch members in the crowd. 'I want that right away,' he bellowed as he grasped the blood red flag, but as he struggled to pull it away, he only succeeded in turning the flag round. Apparently undaunted, Chubb, almost hysterical, screamed out that membership of the federation was a falsehood and Socialism was a 'hydra-headed monster'. The section of the crowd that had come to the meeting out of curiosity laughed but Cobb was far from amused. He told Chubb, in a severe and solemn tone, that if his presence was spotted at any future meeting, he was be 'instantly chucked out'. Observers from the Press commented: 'Mr Chubb will not be able to renew his efforts to arrest the spread of Socialism; the gaiety of the place will suffer.' The gaiety of Mugsborough seemed inappropriate as a deluge of summonses continued against the barrow-pushers. It was their livelihood that suffered.

CHAPTER 7

COBB FIGHTS BACK

For many Hastings contemporaries it must have appeared that Alf Cobb was taking on the whole local establishment single-handedly. His political colleagues stood in amazement as he pressed on unflinchingly with his planned counter-offensive against those who had dared sanction the tough enforcement of the bylaws covering obstruction. His attempt at reprisal against his arch foe, Councillor Cox, had failed through lack of finance: now he tried to turn the same bylaws against one of the Borough's departments. He issued a summons against the manager of the Entertainments Association for obstructing Carlisle Parade with a platform used for stacking chairs. If successful, this would effectively hoist the Corporation with its own petard. The case was heard in September 1908.

Cobb told the Magistrates, in evidence, that whilst passing the Conservative Club the paper he was reading blew out of his hands and under the platform. He was forced to go down on his hands and knees to retrieve it. As a witness to this highly improbable story, Alf called Albert Sellens (a painter who had once worked for Adams and Jarrett) who confirmed he had seen the platform and considered it an obstruction. Alf stated that he had brought the case in the public interest as the platform protruded over the parade by a foot or more and was obviously an obstruction. When told a special provision entitled the Corporation to place chairs on the streets and parades, he replied:

> 'I don't think a public body has the right to obstruct a public highway. Anyway, the chairs on the platform could not possibly be for the public use: in my opinion they should be taken away at night and replaced for people to sit on each morning. The hawkers on the beach have to remove their goods and stalls every evening.

The Association's solicitor pointed out that the chairs would cause less obstruction stacked than if left over the parade.

'I think that, with the wealth the Entertainments Association has at its command, they ought to have storage for them,' answered Alf spiritedly.

'Cart them away?'

'Yes.'

Had Cobb seen any traffic obstructed by the stacked chairs?

'It would certainly prevent me from drawing my barrow up to the pavement at that point and I could have picked up my paper comfortably if it had not been in the way'.

Albert Sellens confirmed he had seen Alf's paper blow under the platform. Not surprisingly the Magistrates ruled against any obstruction, although the Chairman, unexpectedly, thought the Association should bear the costs. It was a minor victory. As he left Cobb told the Court he was considering bringing another action soon.

In late September 1908 the two local Socialist parties wrote to the Education Committee urging the need for an early start in feeding impoverished school children. Both letters were passed over without even being recorded on the minutes. Cobb's correspondence was described as 'altogether too dictatorial' and 'bordering on the impertinent'. 'It was not for a handful of individuals to instruct us,' insisted one Hastings Councillor pompously. After it was agreed to pass swiftly onto the next business, a minority of members objected – they thought it was the Education Committee that was now being impertinent. The Clerk had received a letter from the National Union of Teachers. The Hastings Teachers' Conference had decided to give the balance of their funds to charity. It was proposed that £150 should be invested in a Hastings trust fund. The interest should be used to purchase boots for needy children attending the Borough's elementary schools. The Chairman, without a hint of embarrassment, snapped up 'this generous offer with great thanks'. The irony of accepting such an offer with unashamed eagerness fully escaped the Committee members. The trust fund exposed the neglect of the children in the Committee's 'care' and totally vindicated the charges of ineffective action by the Socialists. The teachers had been stunned to witness children running around barefoot in mid winter. The N.U.T. trust fund is still in existence today.

Tom Kennedy made another visit to Hastings in October. He arrived on a day set aside for a nation-wide demonstration demanding the 'Right to work'. Less than half an hour after his train pulled into Mugsborough's ramshackle station, Kennedy was addressing an assembly of unemployed in Wellington Square with Alf Cobb in support. Social Democrats had tramped the town for a solid week urging the workless to attend. Kennedy gave a fierce, uncompromising speech:

> If men are denied the right to work and are reduced to want,
> they have either to accept charity or starve or obtain a living
> by illegal and unconstitutional means; personally I have long
> believed that only fools would starve in the midst of plenty.

Cobb's shorter address was equally fiery. He exhorted the out-of-works to rise in their might and sweep the Government and the governing classes out of existence. It was in the interest of the ruling class to keep them down and maintain an army of unemployed. He called Asquith 'a liar and a thief.' Tom Kennedy was later accused of deliberately inciting the unemployed to riot and lawlessness. He told a press reporter: 'If it is right to tell women to riot to get the vote, it is equally as reasonable for Socialists to advocate that the underfed working classes should riot for bread.'

It is hard to accurately gauge the success of this Wellington Square assembly for the right to work. One Hastings newspaper regarded it as 'an utter fiasco' and a 'depressed and melancholy looking gathering':

> One looked in vain for the genuine unemployed in the small
> crowd of errand boys, curious passers-by and the few loafers
> who looked on with their hands in their pockets and seemed
> quite oblivious of what was going on.[20]

The *Hastings Observer* reported that the Socialist resolution in favour of the right to work brought a positive response from only seven people 'including the speakers and the banner bearers who put up their hands'. Despite this poor response, Cobb despatched a telegram to the mass demonstration in Trafalgar Square declaring that the resolution had been carried unanimously. Jack Williams, who was tried for sedition after the West End Riots of February 1886, read out Cobb's telegram to the London assembly. Williams commented afterwards: 'There's a beautiful town for you to sack.'

Kennedy did criticise an article he had seen in the *Hastings Pictorial Advertiser* as an attempt to belittle the meeting, it was something the Socialists must expect from the local press; it was full of untruths and misstatements. Press coverage probably exaggerated the 'Fiasco in Wellington Square'. Yet a local paper that had covered the demonstration made no attempt to hide the success of Kennedy's Sunday evening meeting 'attended by considerably over a thousand persons'. The Social Democratic campaign supporting the unemployed lasted a full week. Cobb condemned a recent decision by the Distress Committee to defer an appeal for funds until the numbers of those out of work could be estimated. In mid-October he led a deputation of unemployed workmen into the Council Chamber. The Chief Constable, anticipating trouble, placed police constables at the Town Hall entrance. Several plain clothed and uniformed men took up positions in the vestibule and upper corridors. The deputation was heard at the conclusion of Council business. Alf expressed his dissatisfaction that the Council had shelved the question of unemployment by referring a six-week-old resolution to the Distress Committee. He complained of the Committee's decision not to appeal for public subscriptions until the men had registered. He noted that two councillors supported a resolution pressing the Government to cultivate wastelands and referred to the Sports Ground and Pilot Field, both owned by the Board of Guardians. The Corporation had lost £14,000 by letting the Sports Ground to a private company; that sum should have been spent on the unemployed. He indirectly accused the Mayor of cowardice by not suspending the Standing Orders so that the question of unemployment could have been first on the agenda for the afternoon. The Mayor protested: 'You have no right to say that.' Cobb then pointed an accusing finger at Councillor Butler: 'I am told to 'drop it' but I am here to express my opinions.' He demanded that the Council take immediate action to relieve distress – the total income of the Distress Committee was quite insufficient, averaging less than a shilling a week for those in need. Perhaps the Mayor could make a statement to the Deputation on the Council's intentions? The Mayor was caught unawares: The Distress Committee Chairman is not here.' He glanced anxiously around the Chamber and asked if any member of the Council wished to say anything. Nobody came to his assistance except the Town Clerk who stated rather lamely that the Committee was doing everything possible to alleviate the distress. 'No, sir,' shouted Cobb emphatically.

The Deputation came away empty handed. The Mayor's assurance that everything in the Council's power would be done for all those out of work sounded hollow and complacent.

CHAPTER 8

HARRY HYNDMAN VISITS HASTINGS

One day in early December, 1908 the local Social Democrats took the unprecedented step of hiring the prestigious Royal Concert Hall for an evening to celebrate the occasion of a visit to Hastings of the membership's star attraction, Harry Hyndman, the long serving national President of the Federation.

The veteran Hyndman had an extraordinary background (for a leading socialist) as a wealthy radical gentleman cricketer and stockbroker. He had read Marx and become devoted to the class struggle. He founded the Federation in 1881 committing the movement firmly in a Marxist direction. Autocratic and deeply sarcastic in nature, Hyndman's lack of tact had alienated Marx so that both he and Engels regarded Hyndman with contempt and dismissed his organisation as sectarian. His Jingoism, anti-Semitism and hatred of Germany mixed oddly with his fervent revolutionary socialism.

In January 1886 Hyndman and John Burns led a large procession of unemployed towards Trafalgar Square where a Fair Trade meeting was in progress. When the leaders of the demonstration were turned away by police they marched up Pall Mall in the direction of Hyde Park. As they passed, the marchers, reacting to taunts and jeers, stoned the windows of the exclusive Pall Mall clubs. Hyndman, wearing a frock coat and top hat, was one of four S.D.F. leaders arrested to face prosecution and acquittal.

This controversial figure, smug, tactless and sardonic, could not fail to draw the crowds in Mugsborough that December evening. The Rev. Jamieson, pastor of Park Road Wesleyan Church presided. It was his first appearance on the S.D.F. platform. Securing the services of a local minister as president was a small triumph for the branch and an open declaration of Jamieson's socialism. Unwittingly, the organisers of a du Cros Ball two days before had left the Hall partly decorated so that a festive atmosphere prevailed for the packed audience.

Hyndman was short in stature and wore a long beard. He looked much younger than his sixty-six years. His speech was eloquent, rapid and forceful, punctuated by a caustic wit and gentle irony. He climbed the platform to loud cheers and began by reminiscing on the old days when he and other socialist orators were frequently pelted with cabbage stalks, rotten eggs and other missiles: 'I stand upon this platform as a revolutionary Social Democrat, but I, alone, can not make the revolution.' He commented wryly on the fuss being made over the religious question in schools and advocated secular teaching by the State:

> It's a hard job to look after ourselves in this world, without worrying about the next – the State has nothing to do with the afterlife, it cannot have any influence there.

When he painted a picture of starving children in London, a loud cry of 'Shame' was heard coming from the rear of the Hall:

> Oh, yes, I am always hearing that cry, I even know how to spell it. As a matter of fact it is shame upon you. There is a lot of humbug. I humbug, thou humbug, thee humbug, we humbug, you humbug, they humbug; that seems to be the system of the present day. If the authorities can get their end by humbug, there is no need to resort to violence.

'Humbug is cheap – and you like it,' he snapped, to yells of protest.

Hyndman came to the conclusion that most of the audience did not believe him when he spoke of the terrible conditions in the industrial towns:

> What do you know about life in industrial areas, you, who live in this lounger town where those who have made their wealth are good enough to come down and patronize you?

A dissenting voice shouted out 'Nonsense' after he had called the workers in England slaves:

> You stop selling your labour tomorrow and see how many holes you have to make in your belt in a short time.

He went on by comparing the capitalist to a wolf. It was quite true that he worked hard: that he worked very hard and at nights. The wolf also worked hard and worked o'nights. 'But,' he cried,' the harder he works the worse it is for the poor sheep.' He satirised the turn-and-turn-about system of government:

> Tired of the Tory, put in the Liberal; tired of the Liberal put in the Tory; Caesar and Pompey, Pompey and Caesar; pot

and kettle, kettle and pot. There's not much difference, but I think the Liberal is the pot, who is the jackass I will leave you to discover.

His sarcastic barbs were having effect. A voice rose in protest after he advocated the removal of the landlord. He retorted: 'Oh we have got a little landlord down there have we – he owns as much earth as will go into a flower pot.'

At length Hyndman found himself with a sheaf of question papers and remarked that he had no intention of remaining there until three in the morning. One questioner wondered why the placards about the room referred to John Burns as 'Judas Iscariot'. 'He betrayed the cause of the people,' answered Hyndman to yells, protests, cheers and boos.

John Burns had once been the most militant leading members of the Federation. Burns, Tom Mann, and Ben Tillett led the great dock strike of 1889. Burns' role was crucial to the strike's successful outcome:

Conspicuous with his black beard and white straw hat, he led a great procession of the striking dockers round the City of London. There were forty-one banners, some no more than red flags on poles, but some stranger. There were stinking onions, old fish heads, and indescribable pieces of meat stuck on spikes, to show the City magnates what the dockers had to live on. Each day the processions were repeated, growing larger and larger, and commonly ending in Hyde Park.[21]

These processions brought in sufficient subscriptions to prevent the strikers yielding through starvation.

Soon afterwards John Burns grew disenchanted with the politics of the revolutionary left. He left the S.D.F and entered Parliament as an independent Labour member for Battersea in 1892. He later referred to the Federation as 'cranks, fools and faddists who persisted in the unfruitful pursuit of class war and revolution.' By 1906 he had become President of the Local Government Board in the Liberal Cabinet.

The evening at the Royal Concert Hall was concluded with the Socialists singing the Red Flag. This rendering was drowned out by a number of rowdy youths at the back of the Hall who competed by singing the National Anthem while the remainder of the audience quietly vacated their seats.

CHAPTER 9

MUDDLE, MISMANAGEMENT
AND MONSTROUS SCANDALS

A few months after Hyndman's invitation to Hastings the Social Democrats broadened their local campaign. Their candidate, E.P. Edwards, became the first branch member to contest a council ward. The bye-election of March 1909 for the St. Clements and Halton Ward was caused by the death of Councillor Idenden. Edwards gained 86 votes against his Tory and Liberal opponents.

The election campaign was remembered for a sensational article that appeared in a specially produced local issue of *Justice*. The article's heading *Muddle, Mismanagement and Monstrous Scandals of the Hastings Town Authorities* pulled no punches. Mugsborough's Tory Press chose to ignore its detailed allegations of corruption and ineptitude despite the widespread outrage and indignation it caused. However the Liberal *Weekly Mail and Times* was not so coy. It published extracts professing shock and profound outrage at 'this crude indictment' and 'foul' and indiscriminate libel of our public men'. The editor claimed that the publication's 'childish and malicious assertions – avowedly in search of scandal were unscrupulously unfair and inspired throughout with mischievous purpose'. But some Councillors interviewed afterwards took a different view. They supported part of the Socialists' criticism and reluctantly admitted the article's accuracy. It contained several damaging charges against the Corporation and Board of Guardians, concluding that the:

> Hastings local authorities would appear rotten to the core. Where one does not find jobbery and robbery, one finds gross mismanagement. Where one does not find the latter, he will find scandal.

Singled out for scathing criticism were the purchase of the Brisco Estate in 1902 and the Council's acquisition of the Electric Light Company in 1898.

In April 1902 the Town Council had purchased eleven and a half acres of land. The land belonged to the late Miss Brisco's estate in Bohemia. The Corporation bought the ground ostensibly to erect municipal buildings and a winter garden, with the provisional option of widening the roadway alongside and incorporating the White Rock Gardens. For years the construction of a Kursaal or Winter Garden was deemed vital and absolutely necessary to attract visitors. Before the purchase of the Brisco Estate Alderman Tuppenney could scarcely contain his delight at the offer for sale: 'Something wonderful could be done with it'. He was positive that the price asked, £20,000, did not represent the true market value – the land would be a gold mine to the ratepayers if it were built on instead of merely yielding the present agricultural rates. Another Councillor was equally enthusiastic. He was certain that if the Estate was put on the market it would fetch £3000 an acre – they must seize the opportunity of purchase. Yet by 1908 the Brisco Estate remained virtually untouched and Councillors were suggesting that the ground should be sold off at a substantial loss. The special edition of *Justice* printed in Hastings, and almost surely masterminded by Alf Cobb, recorded their re-evaluation:

> The worthy Councillors who had some years previously waxed eloquent of the glorious advantage that they had obtained for the town; came again before the public and assured their poor silly dupes – the townspeople – that it would be in the best interests of the town to resell it for £8000...

Councillor Stace, reacting to the allegations of the *Justice* article, commented: 'I am against selling (the Brisco Estate) for £8000. I think that there is some occult influence at work somewhere.' The interviewing journalist reported that Stace concluded these words 'with a slight droop of the upper lid of the left eye'. Two weeks later questions were raised in the Council Chamber. Who bought the Brisco Estate – who were the agents – who acted as solicitors – how many of the present Council were members when the purchase was sanctioned?

The transfer of the Electric Light Co. from private hands into the ownership of the Corporation aroused deep opposition at the time and suspicion in many quarters. Opponents of the Council acquisition were particularly jubilant to read a report from a Professor Robinson. Robinson had been commissioned by the Public Lighting Committee to set a valuation on the works. He valued the Company's plant and goodwill at £40,000. This estimation was at least £20,000 lower than the price the Corporation had negotiated before the Electric Light Company was wound up in February 1899. But Robinson's report was disregarded. Even the advice of the Borough Engineer was ignored. The Council happily shelled out £20,000 more than their own self-appointed expert had advised as a fair price.

The *Justice* article revealed that Company shares with a face value of £100 were easily obtained at local auctioneer's offices for just £7.10s before the transfer of ownership. These shares were immediately withdrawn as the agitation for the public purchase mounted: 'Negotiations were opened, which resulted in the town paying over £60,000 for the concern so that £100 shares which could not find purchasers at £7.10s became worth £120.' When asked to comment Councillor Stace remarked:

> Of course there is a great deal in the article with which I agree. I remember when the Electricity Works were purchased I brought a motion forward that the purchase be not proceeded with; but then I found the purchase had already been signed by the Old Corporation, then when we got the property we had to replace the mains because they were rotten, put in new machinery because the old was obsolete and practically rebuild the works, which were then too weak to stand the vibration of the new and increased machinery.

The plight of the Electric Light Company had always been in sharp contrast to the hugely successful and privately owned Gas Company. Its shares had stood for many years at a high premium. To increase profits and avoid a local coal tax, the Directors had decided to shift the Gas Works to a new site on unoccupied land lying outside the borough boundary, between West St. Leonards and Bexhill. This was hardly a desirable adjunct to the sea frontage but it made good economic sense. The Corporation-owned Electric Works came into direct competition with a well-established and profitable Gas Company. The Gas Company not only had many Councillors as shareholders but also on its Board of Directors. This clash of interest was referred to in the article. The anonymous author pointed out::

> That the interests of those in connection with the Gas Company are too strong in the Council to allow the (town's electricity) department to be worked successfully.

The author also indicated that Council members were former shareholders in the disbanded Electric Light Company. The scandal crops up in Tressell's novel. Tressell well knew that the Hastings ratepayers had been foisted with a bankrupt Company with clapped out plant. The 'Brigands' are private shareholders in Mugsborough's Electric Light Works. To avoid liquidation they conspire to sell out to the municipality's ratepayers. Sweater discusses the appointment of 'an expert engineer down from London' by the Public Lighting Committee:

> I know a man that will suit our purpose admirably – we'll pay him a trifle and he'll say whatever we tell him to – and we'll

rush the whole business through before you can say 'Jack Robinson'.[22]

The *Justice* article then switched its attack to the Board of Guardians: 'One has not to probe very deeply to discover scandals there':

> We will content ourselves with a short statement of one very glaring scandal ... Thirty two acres of land were obtained to build a workhouse thereon; after vast and useless expenditure of public money, this was knocked on the head, because a workhouse would lower the tone of the neighbourhood. An architect – of course a local one – received £4000 for plans and not a single brick was laid. Something near that sum was also wasted on the futile efforts of a water diviner.

The possession by the Guardians of this 'white elephant in the shape of the Elphinstone Road site' was reported in the local press in September 1901. The report showed that 18 acres of land purchased for a new workhouse had never been built on, at a cost to the ratepayers estimated at £14,000.

The Entertainments and Amusements Association also came under heavy fire from Alf Cobb and his colleagues:

> The Association is cute and damnably so. It prevents criticism by co-opting to its ranks three editors of three local papers. Your criticism, if sent, does not appear in the correspondence columns – only, or mostly those that are favourable appear. Hastings Council possesses some members who must lie awake many nights puzzling their heads how to drive through the Local Government Acts. One member declares he can, without leaving his bed, switch on the electric light, thereby being able to read in bed. Possibly he conceived this idea because what he thought of in bed he forgot in the morning, whereas now he is enabled to table his ideas as soon as they occur to his mind. Herein, perhaps lies the secret of his appointment to the chairmanship of the Entertainments and Amusements Association.

Although the abuse against the town's authorities caused great local rancour and public indignation it was significant perhaps that no damages were taken out for libel.

CHAPTER 10

THE COUNTER-SOCIALIST DRIVE

As the storm over the Socialists' sweeping charges of municipal corruption and mismanagement abated, orders were issued to place Alf Cobb under close police observation, Summonses for obstruction of the highway, commonly for trivial and fatuous bylaw infringements, became a recurring and tedious feature of his life.

One of the many examples of this petty victimisation occurred in May 1909 after Alf had briefly left his barrow unattended outside a butcher's shop at the corner of King's Road and Cross Street, St. Leonards. On his return he found his handbarrow under the inspection of a police constable.

'You must want a job,' remarked Alf contemptuously, 'I've only been to pay a bill.'

In Court he vigorously cross-questioned the constable assuring the Magistrates the witness' answers were the reverse of the truth. He asked the policeman if he would report anyone who went into a shop and left a motor-car, bicycle or carriage outside. The constable began his reply: That all depends –' Cobb cut him off with a furious stare: 'That's it: it all depends who the person is.' He maintained that the action against him was instigated by certain unnamed individuals aided and abetted by the private desire of a policeman to have a morning's holiday attending court:

> No such thing as wilfully causing an obstruction entered my mind. I hope the Bench will dismiss this case and not censure the constable, but ask that in future he should not manufacture charges of this nature against citizens who honestly want to earn a living.

A police superintendent was called to give evidence. He informed the Magistrates that the defendant was allowed to stand outside the 'Old England' pub from four p.m. on Saturday afternoons but 'he generally loitered about taking little notice of police officers' requests.' Cobbs' fate in Court was sealed. After a fine was imposed he thanked the Bench 'for another miscarriage of justice'.

In June 1909 the Town Council instigated an experimental system permitting licensed hawkers to trade on parts of the seashore east of the White Rock Baths. This was a compromise arrangement allowing a designated number of resident hawkers, each wearing an identification badge, to resume trading on the bench. The intention was to reduce the previous summer's proliferation of hawkers' trucks and barrows that had spread to the esplanade at Denmark Place and other adjacent thoroughfares.

A month passed before Cobb was once again dragged before the Borough Bench. Again the offence was trifling. He was charged with obstructing Station Road, Bexhill by placing a mineral-water box on the pavement to use as a makeshift platform for delivering a Socialist address. Two other Hastings socialists were also summoned. As usual Alf conducted his own defence with the obvious disdain and disrespect for the Bench. In his eyes the Courts were instruments of class oppression. He asked the police constable who had intervened:

'Why did you not tell me that I should be charged?'

'I left that to my superior officer.'

'I suppose they don't trust the constables in Bexhill.'

Cobb demanded equal rights with open-air religious meetings. He knew the Salvation Army had previously held a meeting in exactly the same spot in Town Hall Square – they had suffered no such harassment. Before he had any chance to re-examine the witness he was interrupted by the Chairman of the Magistrates: ' Whatever you are saying has nothing to do with the case.'

'You don't know what I am going to say.'

'Stand down and be careful what you say.'

'I'll sit down.'

'Stand down. I tell you.'

'No, I will sit down' responded Cobb, obstinately.

Alf asked for a map of Bexhill to test the evidence. 'You ought to have provided yourself with a copy,' sneered the Magistrates Clerk.

'We did not anticipate anyone coming here manufacturing evidence of this description.'

'You have no right to say that whatever, I have told you once and I won't tell you again,' fumed the Chairman.

'I hope you won't.'

Cobb rested his defence with a shaky legal claim. He argued that since a bylaw permitted religious out of door meetings and Socialists regarded their doctrine as their religion, they must have the same rights as the Salvation

Army. This logic did not impress the Bexhill magistrates, despite Alf's ingenious interpretation of the local bylaws.

Through the summer of 1909 the forward march of Socialism continued. The spread of Socialist propaganda began to make headway amongst a section of working men and destitute poor. This positive response produced alarm and consternation from Mugsborough's propertied class and some evidence of genuine panic by arch Conservatives. John Chubb's correspondence in mid-June hints at this nervousness:

> Are these people to be allowed to carry on their work practically unopposed? I know the real number of the two divisions of Socialists do not number many, but their continual sapping and mining is doing its deadly work upon the minds and feelings of people, who, a short time back, would not hold in with any one of their tenets...
>
> This week a young man is down here for a week's mission and he seems to excel his leaders in denunciations of society in general and abuse of those who dare be in opposition. Then again how is it that these folk defy our bylaws? Monday night it was 9.25pm when they finished and several of their meetings are held on the Parade, as the spot they took at Caroline Place has ceased to be 'The Beach'.
>
> What are the Anti-Socialist League doing to stem the tide? Shall we go to sleep until it is too late for active resistance?[23]

Heed was taken of Chubb's dire warnings. In a matter of days a counter-socialist drive was organised. On the first Monday of July a London Solicitor, named Urwin, addressed a large, partly hostile crowd from an Anti-Socialist Union van, stealing the spot at the Yacht Stade normally occupied by the S.D.F. members. Predictably, Cobb, wearing a bright red tie, was one of the onlookers. He unsuccessfully demanded the right to reply from the platform after Urwin proclaimed that: 'Socialism, to the community at large, meant absolute slavery.' Urwin ignored Cobb's interruption and crassly asked his audience if they were wage slaves. This brought loud shouts of Yes'.

'No you are not because you have absolute freedom.'

A large portion of the crowd burst into laughter. Alf grew more and more frustrated as he was stubbornly refused any chance to speak during the entire evening.

But the Social Democrats were not going to be caught out twice. The next day they arrived early and recaptured their pitch on the beach opposite the Queen's Hotel. Alf Cobb was incensed. He passionately denounced the refusal to allow him the right to reply. When the Anti-Socialists put in an appearance that evening they found the tables turned – they were forced to speak from a box, in close proximity to the Socialists. Their leaders had been forbidden to place the van on the beach again without the Town Clerk's permission.

Only three evening meetings were held at Harold Place by the Anti-Socialists before serious doubts were voiced about the wisdom of this organised opposition. One Tory columnist suspected the upsurge in anti-socialist activity was counter-productive and wondered if the organisers had thought through the consequences of their offensive. He feared the planned resistance would stir the Socialist agitators to intensify their campaign and add to their notoriety.

The journalist's doubts were disregarded. An outdoor debate was soon arranged with the Anti-Socialists on the question 'Is Socialism sound?' The Social Democrats' debating opponent was H. Johnson, the publican of the Angel Hotel, which was situated on the town's West Hill. Johnson, in his younger day, had been a noted I.L.P. orator. Since then his politics had moved dramatically to the right. He described himself as the arch enemy of Socialism. Despite his reputation and background he was no match for Alf Cobb.

The Socialists had accepted a proposal that Councillor Carey, a staunch Conservative, should act as chairman and arbitrator. At the outset Carey objected strongly to the brilliant red covered platform thoughtfully supplied by the local branch.

'I will never stand on that,' he cried, 'you must cover it with a newspaper or something.' When a copy of the *Hastings Observer* was provided for the purpose, Alf took equal exception:

'And I'm not standing on that.'

A compromise was reached after the offending colour was covered with a plank. The press reported a gathering of three or four hundred onlookers, with the local Socialists turned out in force wearing flaming red ties – a 'fanatical' looking younger element were equipped with umbrellas.

There was a lengthy disagreement about who should start the debate. Eventually Johnson gave way, mounted the platform, climbed onto the plank and gave a dispiriting performance: 'You're preaching the gospel of discontent to the working classes.'

The Socialist audience readily agreed with him. His declaration that this discontent was ruining the Empire was met with derisive laughter. When he admitted he was addressing them as a working man, a voice from the back shouted back derisively: 'What, pulling beer?'

Johnson's gravest mistake was to confess that he lacked a full understanding of Socialism. Cobb seized on this error. To roars of delight, he neatly damned Johnson's failure to comprehend Socialist theory:

> How was it possible for anyone to prove something was unsound if he did not understand it? Johnson quotes the Hastings Electricity Works to prove the failure of municipal undertakings, but Hastings is not run by Socialists; and undertakings that are run municipally will not be so refreshingly successful as they might be, so long as your private Gas Company Directors are on the Town Council to mismanage the Electric Light Works.

Johnson became noticeably upset after Cobb made an insulting jibe about the basic iniquities of brewers and publicans. He replied heatedly: 'I have seen strawberries being sold on barrows and the big ones are usually on the top.' (A year later Cobb was summonsed for obstruction. He was selling strawberries from his barrow in the highway.)

Johnson was also unhappy about his opponent's sarcastic references to beer and 'angels'. He complained that this was hitting below the belt. 'What about strawberries?' roared the crowd, to Johnson's discomfort.

The debate was wound up with each speaker allotted ten minutes to sum up. True to form Alf Cobb had the last word:

> Johnson has come with a sledgehammer to pulverize Socialism, but he has only managed to pulverize himself. The spectacle might appeal to my sense of humour but the real question was 'Is Socialism sound?'

He put the question to the vote and secured an overwhelming show of hands. As he sprang off the crude platform, Alf was surrounded by his colleagues who shook his hand, cheered and patted his back.

The local press found the whole episode unfortunate. An editorial noted that while the Socialists were full of ardour and extraordinarily keen, the average citizen opposing them was generally politically unenthusiastic:

> Consequently Socialists turn up in large numbers at every gathering of this kind while their opponents are represented by a miscellaneous crowd which is by no means their equal either in voting power or intellectual ability (or understanding of the subject under discussion). The

> Socialists had naturally turned out in force to see their
> Champion rout the supporter of reaction.[24]

This zeal and enthusiasm was well demonstrated by Cobb the day after the 'unfortunate episode':

> We are going to push forward the aims and objects of
> Socialism during the coming season: we are going to literally
> make things 'hum'.

He urged all those who wanted to squelch Socialism to attend their next meeting to thrash the matter out; to beat them all ends up if they could. Some of the spectators listening to Alf's words approved of 'squelching' Socialism:

'There they are! Glory to Tariff Reform and Toryism; the first sheep baas and all the rest bray,' he exclaimed. If his political opponents had nothing original to bring forward, perhaps they should study anti-socialist literature and then oppose him with that material:

'Socialists court opposition, it is the finest thing in the world,' he announced proudly.

Summonses for obstruction meanwhile kept dropping through his letterbox. In September 1909 he was charged with obstructing Carlisle Parade. Again the offence was piffling. Evidence was provided in Court that his fruit barrow had remained stationary on the parade for seven minutes. He told the Bench it was a clear-cut case of harassment. The Chief Constable made sure to remind the Magistrates that Cobb had twice been fined that year for similar offences. Alf interjected:

'There is a certain amount of political spite between myself and the police constable.'

'Well, he has shown no bias here,' replied the Magistrate's Clerk.

'No, not here, but we get it outside.'

He defended himself in a long statement, reminding the Bench of his past observations on the partisan enforcement of bylaws. People who were fortunate enough to own motor-cars could obstruct the highway as they liked, without appearing in a police court, whilst the owners went into refreshment bars or cafes on the front:

> They are in the happy position of owning motor cars, whilst
> we – we are only hawkers. We have known magistrates to
> take their bicycles on the front to listen to the band to cause
> just the same obstruction as we do. Why shouldn't they be
> summoned for obstruction in the same way as hawkers?

These last comments, though brave and uncompromising, were unlikely to gain him a sympathetic hearing. But then he did not expect it. His request to be allowed to pay the fine in instalments was denied.

The last public debate of 1909 was staged at the Public Hall in November. J. MacDougall, a dour Scot, accepted the unenviable task of defending the Liberal Government's record. A Hastings press reporter recorded that Alf Cobb, 'with his usual flow of oratory, gave a vehement, passionate and witty disclaimer of the Government and all of its works'. Another local newspaper was far more expansive:

> Cobb's sarcasm was much in evidence during the debate. His caustic wit, fluent tongue and apt repartee dominated the meeting. His keen, alert, semi-humorous style was a complete contrast to the heavy, stolid and deadly serious demeanour of his Scottish opponent, whose humour, needless to say was quite lacking.
>
> It was a curious crowd that filled the Public Hall: a motley mixture of Liberals, Tories and Socialists, who cheered, booed, derided and laughed at various points. And Mr Cobb's sparkling wit and ready sallies brought forth many a response from both sides... he got in a blow almost at every opening.[25]

Alf received a great ovation as he rose to speak. He dismissed the Liberal philosophy that the greatest good was shared by the greatest number – it was shared by the few: 'And the Liberals will tell us that it is shared by the landowner.' After Cobb had made a swingeing attack on the Government's past record, an irate protester shouted: 'Why don't you deal with the present time?' Alf turned to him and mildly enquired:

'Is the past of the Liberal Party too black for you to hear, my friend?'

He dared the audience to contradict his belief that the Liberal Party would send men to prison if they stood up for their rights – just as it had imprisoned long ago the leaders of working class movements. At this, scores of Liberals voiced their dissent. Cobb glanced up, surprised at being asked to state the obvious:

> Oh, all right, I'll prove it to you. These gentlemen, these local Liberals who sit on the bench, are they not prepared to send me and other Socialists to gaol for daring to speak in open places?

Many of the audience appreciated Cobb's point, knowing that a Liberal Magistrate was chairing the debate. Liberals, however shouted out 'Rot!'. 'Thank you for your kind and polite attention but keep the rot to yourselves,' he answered.

One member of the audience persistently interrupted. Alf suggested that he should not get too excited:

'There is no need for you to interject, because you will get the worst of it, chummie'.

A woman began to harangue the Socialists' champion instead. Alf, in a gentle remonstrance, asked her to please be quiet: 'I don't mind the others at the back, but I don't want to have to make you look stupid.'

To a chorus of catcalls he told the noisier demonstrators that under the existing Government it wasn't the rich who were heavily taxed but 'simply you poor devils of working men who bore all the taxation and liked it so much.'

MacDougall made a complete fool of himself. The entire audience looked amazed when he accused the Socialists of working hand in hand with the Tory Party. Alf glanced up at his opponent with a tolerant smile. A look of pity spread over his face as MacDougall indicted the Reds with stealing their policies from the Liberals. He quoted the Post Office as an example of State failure of management. Cobb retorted:

> If the condition of the workers in Government employ is not good isn't that the fault of a Liberal Government that had been mostly in power since 1892?

At the debate's conclusion Cobb sought to encourage similar public confrontations with either Liberals or Tories. A challenge thrown down by the Social Democrats three days later for a debate with the Liberal candidate Tweedy-Smith found no response.

CHAPTER 11

MUGSBOROUGH HIGH AND DRY

If the allegations made by the Social Democrats in their article *Muddle, Mismanagement and Monstrous Scandals* were confirmed, then Mugsborough Council had a long history of dipping its fingers deep into other ratepayers' pockets. Included within the compass of the Socialists' scathing criticism of the borough's administration was the Waterworks Department. The Department stood accused of squandering and frittering away public money so that Hastings was left without a satisfactory water system: 'each year expenditure overcasts the income – there was nearly a £52,000 deficit in the year ending March, 1908'.

This accusation of bungling financial incompetence was subsequently supported by a large majority of the Corporation early in 1910. They issued a statement admitting that the security and adequacy of the town's water supply was in danger. This humiliating announcement was made upon the advice of the water engineer and an independent expert.

The reasons for the threatened water shortage can be directly linked to Council indecisiveness twenty years before. In 1891 the Corporation had hesitated to act on the advice of both the Borough Surveyor and an underground water supply expert. They had presented a report in September recommending that if the total water supply was to be obtained from one source, then it must be drawn from a chalk formation. The report argued that a new source was needed because of the town's expansion and should be sought in a chalk and green sand formation near Glynde – no underground supply in the immediate vicinity of Hastings could possibly provide a sufficient volume. While the Corporation dithered and temporised over how to act on this expert advice, Eastbourne Water Company stepped in and selected the very spot recommended by their Borough Surveyor to sink a well. And so Mugsborough lost the potentially cheapest and best source of water to a rival town.

By January 1910 the water question was deeply troubling the Hastings authorities. The temporary water stations that supplied the town were in a critical state and one had broken down completely, cutting off 60,000 gallons per day. There was alarm over the low reservoir stock and the pollution of two sources of supply affected by recent borough extensions.

To overcome the crisis a Parliamentary Bill was promoted to allow the Corporation to secure sufficient borrowing power to fund an increase in the water supply. Should the Bill pass into law it would enable the Council to finance the extensions and development of existing sources of water and to eventually sink wells in Brede Valley. Several other minor clauses in the Bill included a pernicious attempt to restrict all street hawking to licence holders. These licences were to be granted by a Council Committee sitting behind closed doors.

But the Parliamentary Bill was unanimously opposed at a specially convened public meeting. Opponents complained they had no opportunity to study the Bill's main clauses and hinted darkly that they could place no trust in either the elected Corporation or the officials paid so highly for their expert opinion. After the shock outcome of the debate, a local newspaper headline read: 'Ratepayers indifferent to a threatened water famine.' The paper's editorial admitted that the packed hall had shown a disquieting evidence of a wide and obstinate distrust for the town's government:

> This is a severe condemnation, not necessarily of the present town Councillors, but of the government of the town for the past twenty years. Time seems so far to have exposed every important collective action of the Corporation as an error of judgement. The heavy purchase price of the electricity works, the acquisition of the Brisco Estate, not less than the want of foresight which led to the dangerous shortage and insecurity of the water supply which is now reported – facts like these, of which we are continually reminded, have combined to produce a contempt of the Corporation, as a whole, which threatens to seriously cripple the government of Hastings.[26]

Alf Cobb came, more or less, to the same conclusion at the local Debating Society: 'The Council are more fit to run a kindergarten in the nursery that to look after the town's interests.' He went on to suggest the formation of a Hastings Vigilance Society – a non-political organisation free to discuss and deliberate upon all matters affecting the ratepayers' interests.

The authorities were in a tight corner. More in desperation than hope they announced a poll of ratepayers to decide if they should continue with the Parliamentary Bill. Long before the poll took place the Corporations' defeat on the issue was a safe prediction. The votes were counted in February 1910, in near farcical circumstances. A substantial majority voted against any continuation with the Bill. A gang of joyful Old Town fishermen labelled a scroll 'Poor Dead Bill' in tar and gave it a mock sea burial.

Criticism of the town's authorities continued unrelentingly from all quarters. Councillors were so conscious of their deficiencies that a Committee was appointed to enquire into the administration of every department of the Corporation. At a March meeting of the Debating Society, the Town Council was put on trial for past mismanagement. Cobb, in a typical display of wit and irony, scornfully referred to the Councillors present in the Hall as wishy-washy individuals – instead of looking after ratepayers' interests they lined their own stomachs and indulged in free feeds and cheap rides. He abused Council members of the Watch Committee, elected, he alleged, to obtain preferential police treatment for certain individuals. They attended police concerts and suppers and came away 'with the biggest cigars they have ever smoked in their lives':

> Today Hastings was paying for the misdeeds of the Corporation because Councillors wanted to feather their own nests and hush matters up. There is not the slightest doubt that the majority of Councillors have proved themselves to be totally unfitted for the task of carrying on the administration of our town. Out of the forty members I doubt if five are worth walking a step to vote for. Why, I don't think the other thirty five are capable of selling Hastings rock let alone manage the business of the Corporation. And as for the Entertainments Association, that is simply a fraud. It is organised simply and solely for the benefit of a gentleman with the express object of enabling him to sell buns and sweetmeats.

A month later, on April 15th, the Committee appointed by the Council to enquire into Council departmental maladministration made its first report.

CHAPTER 12

COBB PROSECUTES THE HASTINGS MAYOR

AND CORPORATION

As the debt-ridden Waterworks Department limped on into the Spring of 1910, rumours began circulating that the Social Democrats planned to select a candidate to stand at the next General Election. Alf Cobb, S.D.F. Branch Secretary, was asked to comment. He told an enquiring press reporter that educating the masses to the ideals of Socialism was more urgent than working to win the seat, but the Branch had discussed running a candidate, believing the number of Socialist converts was on the increase. When asked why he did not consider standing himself since he was so well known, Cobb replied that his earnings as a fruiterer would immediately drop should he press his political views forward to that extent. Did this mean his earnings were dearer to him than his principles? Alf acknowledged the point with a smile and explained that the prohibitive election expenses would be difficult to raise from the membership of one hundred and fifty.

One possible candidate was S. F. Jones of Fulham – the Social Democrats' first invited guest of the new season. Speculation intensified as Jones began a week's address on April 23rd. The week was dominated by uproar, abandoned meetings and riotous assembly. Jones took delight in goading his audience. He referred to King Edward VII (who was to die shortly afterwards) as 'Teddy' and endlessly repeated this familiarity to screams of protest. In Eric Hobsbawm's study *Labouring Men* the author indicates that the Countess of Warwick was a stalwart of the S.D.F. 'whose personal relations with H.M. Edward VII were of the closest'.[27] And so perhaps Jones had good reason for the familiarity.

He unduly provoked another section in the crowd when he defined England's aristocracy as a 'race of people so bloated that they were not even able to reproduce their own kind'. It took the arrival of a police constable to restore order. The following day a group of Tory youths raised a platform next to Jones' rostrum in Caroline Place and an unknown individual, wearing a long haired wig and flowing moustache, caused further havoc by impersonating the S.D.F. speaker.

At the beginning of July 1910 controversial new bylaws were enforced. These draconian measures outlawed religious and political meetings anywhere on the beach between the Queen's Hotel and the Royal Oak. This effectively excluded any gatherings in the neighbourhood of Denmark Place, a favoured spot for the Salvation Army and the Socialists. Both organisations ignored the restrictions and disputed the Corporation's authority by petitioning Winston Churchill, the Home Secretary. Local journalists anticipated opposition and conflict from both camps. They thought the Socialists' response was likely to be 'anything but peaceful compliance'.

Two religious bodies, the 'Open Brethren' and Captain Cunningham's Church of England service, complied with the new regulations. But Captain Slee of the Salvation Army and Alf Cobb and his comrades stood their ground. Afterwards Slee was interviewed by the press:

> There is only one body whose meetings are not quiet and against them are the complaints levied. There is a clever man at their head, however the Corporation are rather nervous, and there you are – the flock of sheep is slaughtered to kill the wolf.

A prolonged conflict became obvious when Captain Slee announced that it was quite impossible for the Army to abandon that part of the beach since there was not another spot to hold open-air meetings:

> I have had to fight for my pitch on the Stade. It has been continued fighting between us and the Socialists. After thirty eight years we are not going to give up our open-air meetings.

Alf Cobb was determined not only to stand firm but to take reprisals against the beach restrictions. He had old scores to settle with the town authorities. In a move outlandish in its daring, he summonsed the Mayor of Hastings, in his corporate capacity, for breaching the Council's own bylaws by placing the Beach Concert Pavilion on the Fishmarket Stade – space that had been officially allotted for public meetings.

The case was heard before the local Borough Bench on July 21st after the authorities had gained two adjournments amid claims that Cobb was using the Courts for cheap notoriety. At the centre of great excitement Alf

Cobb conducted his own prosecution. The densely packed courtroom was crowded with sympathisers and supporting Salvationists. Alf stood before the Bench and charged the Summer Entertainments Syndicate with erecting a booth on the seashore contrary to existing bylaws. The Magistrates listened in outrage as the Mayor and Corporation were summoned for aiding and abetting.

The Town Clerk represented the Mayor and Corporation – F.W. Morgan appeared for the Syndicate. It was soon apparent to the defence that Alf Cobb had a strong case in law. Morgan was forced to question the validity of the bylaws. He admitted in Court that the logical conclusion to their full implementation would have prevented the building of the Harbour Offices, the Fish Packing Shed and even the Pier on the beach. Alf agreed with Morgan – the bylaw proviso was bad, but it was 'quite fitting that the Council, with its usual wisdom, should exceed its powers'. He cited it as an instance where the Corporation were prepared to run a coach and pair through their own bylaws. After he labelled the Town Council and its representatives 'shufflers', the Chairman interrupted him:

'We cannot have that in this Court. Keep to the point and we will listen to you. It is not a proper remark.'

'Proper remarks soon become improper here.'

'So long as you make remarks of this kind you must not expect the sympathy of the Court.'

'You mean that if I make improper remarks the Bench will forget the justice of the case and deal with it differently?'

'I did not say that.'

'Then I have nothing to fear.'

The Magistrates retired. On their return the Chairman read out the verdict:

> We have come to the conclusion that we must sustain Mr. Morgan in his argument that the bylaw is ultra vires and unsustained by the powers of the Act of 1895. Both summonses will be dismissed without costs.

Cobb made a further application to the Bench. He considered the performances at the Beach Concert Pavilion interfered seriously with the holding of meetings at the Fishmarket. He complained of the noise of the piano, the singing and the applause. It was no longer possible to hold meetings at the Yachts. During the next month they wanted to hold a series of meetings at the Fishmarket.

'As friends we should advise you not to hold such meetings,' responded the Chairman smiling.

'Such friendly advice I shall be unable to accept. I should rather think the means lay in the removal of the building in question.'

Alf withdrew.

All through July, whilst Alf Cobb prepared his prosecution against the Corporation for breaking its own regulations, the Salvation Army Captain continued steadily to hold his meetings at the forbidden Yacht Stade pitch. As news spread he was under sentence of imprisonment his audience grew larger. Some observers suspected Captain Slee was eager for martyrdom.

The local Liberal weekly condemned the new regulations as 'bad' in law and nonsense in practice. The paper considered the Corporation had brought local government into an atmosphere of 'comic opera'. The ineffective legal steps were too absurd for serious fiction but might be tolerated in farce:

> The conclusion is unavoidable, that the steps taken by the Corporation in exercising beach control are in the direction of mismanagement. They know neither their own weakness nor the strength of their opponents and the measurement has led to public discomfiture. Future procedure must be by negotiation...[28]

A measure of the Salvation Army's defiance was given on Sunday, July 10th. The Army ignored the warning of the Watch Committee not to hold religious meetings on the Queen's Stade foreshore and held services there morning, afternoon and evening. The S.D.F also defied the law that day with an address from Mr. Butler, its guest speaker from Pimlico. Butler protested that the Corporation was trying to snatch away the rights of free, unfettered speech – the beach was public property. Why should Socialists be asked to forego their rights by accepting a code of rules which trampled on their liberties?

On the following Wednesday evening the beach regulations were brought into absolute ridicule. A Nonconformist preacher had arrived in Hastings on a day's excursion together with two hundred followers. He was ordered off the beach at Denmark Place. After the new bylaws were explained to the incredulous minister, he hired a boat at the Queen's Stade and conducted his service from the water. His congregation prayed and sang hymns from the water's edge. The police were powerless to intervene since there was nothing in the bylaw provisions prohibiting meetings either conducted on the water or in it. He told his audience that if he was to preach regularly out of doors in Hastings he must invest in a pair of sea-boots.

In the last days of that memorable July, the London General Secretary of the Social Democratic Party, H.W. Lee, visited Hastings. The visit had a specific purpose – to seek an interview with the Town Clerk, Ben Meadows, about the restrictions on beach rights. Alf Cobb met him at the dilapidated sheds, masquerading as a railway station, and showed him the pitches under dispute, pointing out that several of the allotted spots were covered by water at high tide. Lee informed Meadows that unless the Corporation came to terms with the local branch they were determined to repeatedly test the validity of the bylaws by following the example set by the Salvation Army. The Social Democrats were also preparing a manifesto to be launched locally and then published nationally in *Justice*. The branch was appealing for funds and requesting outside lecturers to deliberately challenge the ruling. Meadows lamely replied that he could do little more than carry out the Corporation's instructions. This could hardly satisfy Cobb. He and other Socialist representatives declared their intention to promote a programme designed to challenge the regulations by inviting new speakers each week. There would be a total refusal to pay any fine. Speakers were prepared for imprisonment if the Council insisted on enforcing sentences.

These threats plus a public appeal by the Salvationists brought a period of truce. Many Councillors were privately worried about how they could escape with dignity from their ill-advised position. The Salvation Army henceforth held regular meetings at the prohibited sites without interference. A series of outdoor meetings by the S.D.P. at the Yacht Stade also went unchallenged.

One month after an uneasy peace was declared, Alf Cobb assailed the town's authorities in a witheringly satirical piece of correspondence. He began by decrying the pitiful sight of numerous working men standing outside the Borough Bench to answer summonses for non-payment of rates. He wondered how many of these men considered they had ever received a fair return for their rate payments. He damned the Council for the appalling upkeep of the roads. Middle Street, where Cobb was then living, was covered with sticky mud when the weather was wet and when dry passers-by were half blinded by dust:

What is true of the roads is equally true with regard to each and every department of Municipal life. In its Council, mess, muddle and mismanagement hold sway. No one but on seldom occasions has the courage to protest against the infernal rot which set in long ago and remains today. All are eager to smother up the faults of each other; this extends from individuals to committees and from the latter to the Council...

Take again the local Police Force, which is considerably overstaffed. To the ordinary person, a police force exists to preserve the peace, yet locally the majority of 'cases' are not real cases of breaches of the 'peace' but are paltry charges that any self respecting and reliant community would deem too ridiculous to proceed with.

A police constable goes on 'duty', that is to say when he is not conversing with his friends; he is keen eyed, vigilant, a man with a mission, he has received – 'instructions'. He has eager sense of smell, of evil smelling motors? – No. He has a piercing glint in his eye for stationary carriages? No; for unattended motor cars? No; for a carriage with flying emblems in which is seated some ladies, who are stationary, offering for sale 'Votes for women', … Oh bless you, no. Why he is laughing, he enjoys this. In fact, if you converse with him on the subject, he will tell you motors, etc, cannot cause obstruction. They are different.

Look at him now, he has stopped laughing, his head is thrown up, he looks this way and that. He has smelt – 'beer' did you say? Oh, no, not that, but good succulent fruit. Ha, ha, thinks he, I must hide. The crowd round the Punch and Judy man is convenient. He pretends he is enjoying it. Ha, that hawker has finished serving a customer. Policeman straightens himself, he no longer needs to hide; he wishes the hawker to know he is about now. Out comes his book and pencil, he has caught a dangerous criminal. This criminal must be taken before the Bench; they are sure to convict, unless the hawker is lucky just once in a while – and gets off. He is fined possibly a sum greater than that which he has earned on the day in question. He loses a day's work attending court. The policeman chuckles when he meets him outside and declares he will have him again. He is delighted with himself; his chums envy him; he is a step nearer promotion; and over and above all, he has justified the existence of so many policemen in Hastings. This means higher rates. 'Tut, tut, man and look pleased.'

This is miles, very many miles, outside the realms of justice. Perhaps Hastings people will become wise. Perhaps in November next they will make up their minds to return to the Council men who are pledged to remove the disabilities under which so many suffer. Perhaps, too, if illegalities are committed all who commit them will be made to suffer and not the hard struggling few.[29]

The Socialists continued their meetings at the stand on the beach opposite the Fishmarket throughout September. Periodically they and the Salvationists persisted in maintaining their beach rights at Denmark Place. Near the Lifeboat House opposing factions of Tariff Reformers and Anti-Socialists kept up their opposition addresses and propaganda.

At a shorter autumn evening session an unusually large crowd gathered to hear Richard Greenwood speak on the class war. In a note to *Justice* Alf Cobb refers to Greenwood's series of ten lectures during his stay in Hastings. He reported the presence of the Anti-Socialist League over the previous two months: 'the League was very discreet, all our efforts to draw them into questions or opposition failed.'[30]

Cobb's disappointment at the branch's failure to draw the League into political debate is expressed in a locally published letter:

> I wonder when the anti-Socialist lecturers will have sufficient courage of their convictions to allow a Socialist the opportunity of criticising their many remarks and rebutting their many misstatements from their own platform?
>
> Better still, when will they accept the challenge of the Socialists to debate? Every opportunity has been offered them in this direction ... We are prepared to give away weight, to use a sporting phrase, and to beat our opponents. To attempt to reply to their multitude of untruths, through your columns would take up more space than it would be possible to allot, but if they care to attend our next or any meeting we shall be holding, I can assure them ample opportunity will be afforded them to question our speaker and if they feel fit, to oppose Socialism. Hoping they will get their pluck high enough up to accept this offer.[31]

CHAPTER 13

FORTY THIEVES LESS ONE?

Alf Cobb's exploits in Court and his battle to preserve ancient beach rights during the summer of 1910 substantially enhanced his standing as a notorious local celebrity. Should the Social Democrats field a candidate in the forthcoming November Municipal elections, there was only one logical choice. The Branch announced its intention to re-contest the St. Clements and Halton Ward, conscious that its high density of slum dwellings provided a fertile political ground. Alf Cobb issued his first election address in mid-October.

At first it was understood that three candidates would contest the Ward, but Councillor Butler announced his withdrawal in suspicious circumstances. Local Socialists regarded this move as very dubious as it left F.W. Morgan, a Hastings solicitor, as Cobb's single opponent. Morgan had defended the Summer Entertainment Syndicate in Cobb's Court action against the Corporation. He was a well to do Tory, obsessed with cutting rates. However, against Alf Cobb, he disassociated himself from any other political party and stood, ostensibly, as an independent candidate. Cobb and his Socialist colleagues saw it differently. Alf bluntly claimed that the local Liberals and Tories had colluded to sink their differences to secure his defeat and 'run a prominent townsman and solicitor, the nominee of the Ratepayers' Association and a Municipal Reformer.'[32] Butler's withdrawal undoubtedly aided Morgan's cause. He had the solid backing of the Ratepayers' Association and was noted as one of its most determined leaders.

Alf Cobb threw himself into the task of winning the seat with unmistakable zeal. The Social Democratic membership rallied to his support. The Fishmarket neighbourhood was transformed into a scene of frenzied activity and lively debate. Cobb rented a Committee Room in the Old Town High Street, covering it with pages from the Party's London journal. Journalists reluctantly admitted that it would not be through lack of hard work if he failed to achieve victory on November 1st. The *Hastings Observer* acknowledged that he did not believe in 'sailing under false colours but stood as an avowed Socialist'. The paper confessed that Cobb was a man of 'some ability and a ready speaker'. The opening paragraph of his election address read as follows:

> Life for the great mass of the people is one long endless round of struggle to live, from which there is no permanent escape other than by Socialism. Much, however, can be done by our local administrative bodies to smooth the rugged path over which the workers have to travel. Our object is to obtain for them the best possible conditions under existing circumstances. The only hope our class have to better their lot is to use their intelligence in their own interest by first, understanding the value of the vote; second using it in their own interest; third refusing to give it to any candidate or party upholding the present system. We Social Democrats are men and women, who, having been trained in the university of life, know how to get value for our money.

At the beginning of October the local Tramway Company employees had pledged themselves to oppose any council candidate who rejected their demands for an overhead trolley system on the front line. This would replace the existing 'Dolter' system that consisted of live electric studs embedded in the road surface. The Dolter system was either faulty or constantly breaking down, endangering public safety and threatening to electrocute any horse passing by.

The Tramway employees condemned the Corporation's insistence on a seafront Dolter system and urged the voting public to support candidates that preferred the safer but unsightly 'overhead' trolley lines. At an open-air meeting at the Fishmarket, T. Ryan, spokesman for the Tram staff, was asked to air his opinions. He mentioned the St. Clements Ward contest and informed his work colleagues in the crowd that Alf Cobb was the only candidate standing for election that supported their motion for an overhead system. He advised them to vote for Cobb who would make a 'fitting representative in the Council Chamber for that Ward':

> Many Councillors were there not for the benefit of the town but for their own advantage. The Council at present did their business behind closed doors and if Mr Cobb was there they could rely upon him speaking his mind.

Ryan told the onlookers, to applause, that the local Council was a disgrace to England.

Four days after Ryan's declared public support, Alf Cobb gave an open-air address at the bottom of Swan Lane. He managed to mount a chair on sloping ground and spoke to about three hundred people. He received an uninterrupted and attentive hearing. He began his speech by asking rhetorically whether the interests of those who sat on Council were identical to the interests of the working class: 'Of course not, if they attempted to agitate for the working class they would soon find themselves out in the cold.' He contrasted his candidature with sitting Councillors and others putting up for municipal office: 'I have nothing to fear. I am not a man who is likely to walk about with my head under my arm, afraid of having my head punched.' He denied a rumour that he had served frequent periods of imprisonment in the past: 'my first introduction to a police court was in Hastings, an acquaintance forced upon me.' He promised that he would speak his mind inside the Council Chamber despite the presence of the Aldermanic Bench, 'whereon sit so many I loathe and despise'. Should he be elected:

> If any of you Corporation employees, or anyone else, will come to me and let me know of any leakage, you can rest assured that it will be investigated without anyone knowing that you gave me the information. I have heard the Councillors of Hastings termed the 'Forty Thieves'. Well, when I get in, there will only be thirty nine. There is too much camera work in connection with Corporation business, and I intend to make committee affairs public property.

The latest scandal to hit the Hastings Corporation had been the controversial conduct of senior members of the Parks and Gardens staff. A special committee of investigation was ordered to examine the working practices of the Parks Superintendent and Head Gardener, C.W. Kerswell. They were found to have illicitly used large tracts of garden ground to cultivate plants for their own use. Parks and Garden employees were instructed to plant, tend and dig these crops and finally load the flowers and vegetables onto carts. It was the destination of these carts that caused the public scandal. Vanloads found their way into the homes and gardens of town councillors. The Head Gardener became a suitable scapegoat and tendered his resignation. (Robert Tressell refers to this public park scandal in his novel).

When Cobb addressed the crowd in Swan Lane on that Wednesday evening of October 19th, 1910, precariously balanced on his 'chair' platform, a breath of scandal was already in the wind. As long as Hastings voters returned men of 'a certain stamp', he said, 'they must look out for such occurrences: these individuals put up for election, not to represent the ratepayers, but to get something for themselves.' He pointed out the insanitary state of many of the Old Town workmen's dwellings. Owners of much of this property were men who sat on the Town Council. Such men were ashamed to acknowledge ownership, yet had the impudence to suggest they worked for the town's interest:

> They live and thrive and leave satisfactory fortunes when they die, through you living in their hovels. If the whole of the Council Chamber combine to prevent me speaking they will not stop me. And if the Chief Constable and his men are brought in it won't make a jot of difference. The Mayor has a little bell with which he is supposed to maintain order. Well, there might be occasions when it is not my duty to observe order, even if I have to mount the table to make myself heard – the Mayor will find I have a bigger bell than his.

Alf Cobb could not have stood for Council election as an undischarged bankrupt. Opponents would soon have brought this knowledge to the authorities' attention. Three weeks before the date of the municipal election he applied to the County Court for his discharge. The case was heard before he announced his candidature. Asked by the Judge why he was making his application now, Alf answered, 'I have a berth offered me I am anxious to accept – that of a fruit and flower buyer, but the firm require a guarantee. That guarantee can only be obtained from a Guarantee Society, who would not give it to me without a discharge.' This unlikely tale was accepted by the Judge. The judgement opened the way for his nomination. Ironically, F.W. Morgan, who was to be Alf's only opponent in the Council Ward contest, acted as his solicitor in the Hastings County Court.

On the last Wednesday evening of October, Morgan courageously accepted Cobb's challenge for a public debate. The Market Hall was densely packed with the St. Clements Ward's electorate – men stood rows deep at the rear and along the side gangways, even jamming the staircase leading to the Hall. The lot fell on Cobb to open the debate. In his speech, which was limited to ten minutes, he complained that Morgan's election address had not disclosed his policy; instead it was full of vague statements and a cautionary word about the upward trend of local rates. When Morgan rose to answer he thanked his opponent for giving him an opportunity to pull his programme to pieces. The 'independent' candidate held up a reproduction of Millais' picture, 'Bubbles', as an illustration of Cobb's electoral address. The painting, said Morgan, was an example of Cobb's boyhood before he was troubled with the alphabet. Now his programme was full of bubbles.

As soon as Alf returned to the platform he hijacked Morgan's 'bubbles' theme. He glanced at his watch and looked over at his opponent: 'ten minutes gone and not one bubble pricked,' he observed, 'the audience will remember "Sapolio Soap", it did not wash clothes but neither will Mr Morgan's policy suit the electors.'

He went on to admonish the County Court solicitor and his fellow lawyers for helping to frame the defeated local Parliamentary Bill. He asked:

> What are my bubbles? Abolishing slums? Supporting public baths and washhouses? Feeding underfed schoolchildren? Mr Morgan has told the audience that he didn't advocate public washhouses – that when he was a child he washed in the kitchen and put his 'tootsies in a bowl'.

Alf turned to his opponent and told him there was another advertisement by 'Pears' – 'Oh, you dirty boy!' He called Morgan a true blue Conservative with a dull and thick head. If Morgan wanted to prick his bubble he would need more than a hatpin but rather a pickaxe.

Morgan was rattled. He complained about the loud hisses and interruptions and the evident lack of fair play. Cobb was anxious to be a Councillor only to advertise Socialism. He would turn the Council into a bear garden.

'Well,' answered Alf, 'it has been a bear garden ere now and the Councillors had the buns – my duty will be to make sure they pay for their own buns.' The day belonged to the hawkers' champion; the ratepayers' hero was vanquished.

Alf's colleagues and supporters confidently anticipated victory. The local branch forwarded an optimistic report to *Justice:*

> Our candidate has already received promises of support from nearly half the voters in the Ward he is contesting: so that unless something extremely unlikely happens he will be the first S.D.P. town councillor in Hastings.[33]

The Social Democrats were heartened because Morgan's campaign appeared to be floundering. A meeting supporting his candidature at Halton was sparsely attended; only enlivened by Cobb's presence, together with a handful of opposing Socialists.

They subjected Morgan to a barrage of heckling. Later the arch Tory, John Chubb, protested about an item in Cobb's Committee Room window which had caught his eye:

> It states on a card 'Why have forty thieves? Why not reduce the number by voting for A. J. Cobb'. Sir, is this not libellous to stigmatise forty gentlemen who give their free time without fee or reward to serve us, as thieves?[34]

Chubb did not classify cartloads of flowers and vegetables as reward!

When the results were declared the Socialists' confidence was sadly misplaced. Morgan won by the narrow margin of thirty-three votes: 394 to 361. A vast crowd of several thousand had gathered in Queen's Road to await the result. The Town Hall corridors and staircases were thronged. Groans and shouts of dismay greeted the declaration. Alf insisted on a recount of one batch of votes stating firmly that next time he would be first, not second.

As Cobb stepped from the Town Hall, a score of policemen unsuccessfully struggled to hold back the stampede towards him. He was lifted shoulder high, waving a very crushed bowler hat. At this point a brass band appeared. It marched past the Town Hall leading a group of Morgan's supporters. Those leading the procession carried a large white banner with the name 'Morgan' emblazoned on it. The band was playing 'See, the Conquering Hero Comes'. Cobb, still carried shoulder high, joined the rear of the march, supported by a large number of followers. The procession proceeded into Wellington Square where Cobb caught hold of a lamppost and kicked himself free. He climbed up the lamp standard which was sited in the road centre and with one hand holding the post and a flushed face began to vilify his opponent's name.

Afterwards he issued a statement explaining his defeat:

> I attribute it partly to the attitude of Nonconformist Liberals and partly because many promised supporters could not get to the poll, owing to time of work. I understand that in the last three hours the Liberals sent appeals to seventy of their supporters to vote for Mr Morgan.

An unnamed Social Democrat wrote to *Justice:*

> Hastings has been in a great state of excitement. Our branch for the first time engaged in the November elections; we nearly won. It took the combined efforts of the officials, Liberals and Tories, in conjunction with Nonconformists and Churchites to keep him from winning. Our chief candidate, a Tory lawyer, was the strongest candidate they could possibly find. He had resided in the ward for forty years and was directly and indirectly interested with Property in St. Clements. He got in with the aid of all the Councillors of the ward by 33 votes ... Hastings working men and women have awoke.[35]

An editorial in the *Weekly Mail and Times* believed Cobb only lost the battle by carrying his 'welcome criticism and wholesome candour to a point that was objectionable':

> Many would have been glad to see his disintegrating voice in a Council diseased with the clubbable spirit and fear of publicity. His communistic ideas would have been harmless, because isolated and he would have stood against the pressure of officialdom and the dead weight of custom. But he breathed fire and brimstone, so to speak, for the mere pleasure of it.[36]

When Walter Coussens was elevated to the Aldermanic Bench, a second opportunity quickly occurred. The bye-election was called for the West Hill ward of Upper St. Mary's. Cobb's opponent was another Tory, Charles Ridgway, standing, like Morgan, as an independent candidate.

The Social Democrats opened a Committee Room at 6 Manor Road. A local journalist questioned Alf about the forthcoming contest while he was hawking in London Road, St. Leonards. Leaning against his barrow of flowers, he told the reporter the reason canvassers were asking voters to support Ridgway. It was because he had been a railway clerk and had served as a workhouse master for twenty-five years. The story was that he had retired to Hastings and felt he would die unless he found something to do. Alf grinned and suggested he use the electoral plea 'Vote for Ridgway and save his life'.

Cobb's opponents knew how close the last campaign had been in St. Clements. They decided to fight off this second challenge by a strategy of intimidation. Their tactics caused Alf to proclaim publicly that he had collected enough written information highlighting intimidation to assure an interesting enquiry. He maintained he was contesting the bye-election not out of notoriety, position or for personal advantage but because he believed the workers' cause was sacred.

Again he lost by the narrowest of margins – a mere thirty-two votes after a poll of nearly nine hundred constituents. Observers were staggered at the size of the turnout that day (December 6th), even larger than at the November election. A crowd approaching a thousand collected to hear the result announced from the Town Hall balcony. The vast majority were in sympathy with the defeated Socialist candidate. As the result was read out Ridgway did not receive a single cheer and, believing that discretion was the better part of valour, slipped away unnoticed. A supporter that remained told a reporter that Ridgway should have romped home – the result showed that Socialism had become a force that needed to be fought 'tooth and nail'. Once again Alf was lifted shoulder high by enthusiastic colleagues. He was carried through the main streets, where the procession stopped at street corners allowing Cobb to deliver typically fiery rhetoric to enthuse his followers. He was finally borne to the same lamp standard in Wellington Square. He took up a position under the lamp and blamed his defeat on 'independent Committees who only furthered their slum property owners' interests which were not the interests of the working community'. He would rather stand proud in defeat than win with the help of those who had supported the retired 'skilly server'. He denied the local branch was downhearted – they would continue the fight. It was their intention not only to fight Municipal but also Parliamentary elections. The man who represented Hastings (du Cros had been returned at the General Election three days earlier) lived at his ease from the labour of the working class; only a Socialist candidate would be able to shift him.

Scarcely drawing breath he angrily attacked the slanted local press:

> You will recollect sir, your own declaration of opinion a fortnight hence. 'Twas madness to vote for Cobb'. Yet the West Hill contains 428 men and women who were, and are again, prepared to accept the opprobrious terms you are prepared to level at those who support me. It was, as in St. Clement's, the most outrageously slanderous statements which aided in my defeat. Ladies again were conveyed to the poll in a nicely appointed pair-horse carriage, believing me to be an Anarchist. With visions of all the horrible things which the newspapers record ... they hurried to the poll, with the fear that a bomb should convey them in another direction.
>
> Our efforts in future will be used to dispel all the lying statements that have been spread broadcast, and to bring to book the utterers of them. Where those of my opponents and mine differ is that mine happen to be true. Theirs are mean, despicable and untrue.'[37]

CHAPTER 14

COBB LANGUISHES IN SOLITARY CONFINEMENT

The renowned militant dockers' leader, Ben Tillett, visited Hastings in December 1910 at the invitation of the Social Democrats. Tillett had specially travelled from Newport, Monmouthshire, to fulfil his engagement at the Public Hall. Alf Cobb, in his introduction as Chairman, told the audience that their guest had undertaken the long journey from Wales to speak that evening, and without a farthing recompense.

Ben Tillett was a legendary figure in the labour movement and is remembered for leading the fight to secure the 'dockers' tanner'. Only that year he and Tom Mann had formed the Transport Workers' Federation in an effort to unite all transport on land, sea and river into one national body. Two years later in the summer of 1912, Tillett was to lead the dockers in the celebrated prayer 'God strike Lord Davenport dead' after the Port of London Authority's Chairman had stubbornly refused to recognise the recently formed Federation. He was Secretary of the Dock, Wharf, Riverside and General Workers' Union and famed for his role in the great dock strike of 1889 when a bitter confrontation developed with the dock employers over demands for the meagre minimum wage of 6d an hour.

That night, Ben Tillett gave a long lecture on 'The Atrocities of Capitalism' and was rarely interrupted. Earlier Cobb had summarised the speaker's militant background and apologised for the relatively poor turnout indicting the 'Clerk to the Weather'. Alf attacked a number of the leaders involved in the 1889 dispute: 'some of them are now in great and high positions and one is receiving £5000 a year for the purpose, not of relieving us from subjection, but to lead us deeper into the mire'. The last reference was to John Burns, referred to as 'Judas Iscariot' during Hyndman's visit to Hastings in December 1908. Burns had contemptuously disowned his former S.D.F. associates and become a hated figure. His disillusionment with Socialism is clear in a statement made in 1900: 'I am getting tired of working-class boots, working-class brains, working-class houses and working-class margarine'.

Tillett, in his speech, blamed capitalism for the misery and poverty in their midst. He asked a series of rhetorical questions. What did the aristocrat of the present day do? Did he construct his own motor car? Did he build or repair his own house? Did he even make his own dress?

> They toil not, neither do they spin, they did not belong to the tribe of the workers: they could only boast of a long line of ancestors who had, like themselves, neither toiled or spun. And what did the nation do? It gave them all that money could buy, the best pictures, the best music, the best education, the best culture. And yet what ungrateful brutes they are – these capitalists.

In the weeks before Christmas, correspondence started appearing in the press which focused on the Parks and Garden Inquiry report. The anonymous writer asked why the Special Committee of Inquiry was keeping the public in the dark. What had taken place behind those closed doors? Why were the Committee terrified of informing the open Council? Could it be possible that Special Committee members sitting in judgement upon one of their employees (the Head Gardener) had discovered they were also sitting in Judgement of themselves and the rest of the Council?

Cobb reviewed the latest scandal to afflict the Council one Sunday evening at a Socialist meeting in the Electric Theatre, Wellington Place (the site now occupied by McDonald's). Onlookers overflowed the hired room and choked its passages. Everyone knew that cartloads of Alexandra Park produce were off-loaded at Councillors' homes; he said. He named the Council members involved, quite openly. Yes, he understood the law of libel, but since the local S.D.P. branch had proof of each case they were well armed to meet any libel action that might be forthcoming. As for the members of the Corporation concerned, they were already putting their heads together in anticipation of next November's local elections. Liberal and Conservatives would adopt a single candidate specifically to keep Labour and Socialist representatives out: 'the truth is they are afraid of us'. No libel action resulted.

Alf Cobb had strived tirelessly to achieve a political foothold in the Council Chamber, but his energetic promotion of Socialism added to a bruising outspokenness created many enemies. His fervent preaching of a radical alternative society frightened off potential support. T. Ryan, who had initially publicly backed Cobb, as an exponent of the overhead tram lines, quickly reversed his enthusiasm. Tramway Company managers gave Ryan time off work to actively canvass against Cobb's candidature in both the contested council wards. Alf knew that the Tramway managers were largely responsible for his close defeats. He did not forgive or forget.

The simmering hostility between Alf and the Tram Company employers flared up into bitter acrimony in the Spring of 1911 when the Company, with malicious intent, brought a case against him for refusing to pay the full fare in a workman's tramcar. He had insisted that rather than paying the full twopenny fare, his trade entitled him to a workman's half pay – privileges covered by local bylaw provisions. The Company, rather than allow him to be included within their category of artisan, mechanic or labourer, had spitefully seized the chance to haul him before the usual collection of Borough Bench Magistrates. The firm's solicitor later applied to the County Court for the recovery of the lost 2d – an absurd example of petty vindictiveness. Cobb was to be charged at a later hearing with failure to pay for a roll of felt he had carried on top of the tram.

The Court hearing was packed full of Tramway Company staff. Cobb rightly demanded that all the witnesses should withdraw to allow the Clerk to call on their evidence one at a time. The conductor involved insisted that Cobb had not come under his discretionary definition of a working man. Alf replied sarcastically:

> So you do not consider that a hawker is a workman? I suppose it is because you see hawkers walking about with fur coats, gold watches and diamond rings which makes you think they are master men.

The laughter continued when the conductor classified the hawkers' champion as a master man because he worked for himself and travelled everywhere by tram.

Alf hit back with a spirited and witty defence. He submitted that a hawker was in the broadest sense a daily labourer. He cited passages from numerous works of historians and authors and read out various definitions. He quoted a seventeenth century dictionary definition of a labourer as a 'person who is low, vulgar and base.' Since several members of the Bench obviously regarded him as very vulgar, very low and very base, this must prove he was a working man and therefore entitled to half fare. He accused the tram conductor of perjury in a deliberately manufactured case. He warned that if the proceedings were allowed to continue Company Inspectors (Ryan was one), would find themselves replacing him in the dock. This was not to be an idle threat. He continued:

> I believe that it is the employees and the Tramway Company that ought to be standing here in my shoes. I could bring the employees up time after time for overcrowding the trains. The Tramway Company should be brought here for non-compliance with an agreed Council proviso to keep the roads in good condition. Not only have I lost a day's work but the case bears all the hallmarks of vindictiveness.

At one stage the Clerk interrupted the Company solicitor to ask Alf: 'What do you say you are — a mechanic, an artisan or a daily labourer?'

'All three.'

Pearson, the Prosecuting Counsel, read out another definition: 'A labourer is a man who digs or does other work.'

'That's me.'

The case was dismissed. Cobb successfully claimed loss of earnings put at half a crown.

Only four days passed before Cobb was in more trouble. His daughter Florrie, then ten years old, left school for her lunch break and briefly took charge of her father's flower barrow in Cross Street, St. Leonards, whilst he found a public toilet. A police inspector unobtrusively watched the small girl as she innocently sold a bunch of violets to a customer. The inspector knew this 'heinous' act infringed the street trading laws. Cobb was charged with allowing a minor to trade without a street licence. Little Florrie was summoned to appear at the Police Court for unlicensed trading — in total disregard for the effect it might have on a young child. The Mugsborough authorities had sunk to new depths.

In a heated interchange with the Justices, Alf ridiculed the idea that a ten-year-old could understand a summons that was difficult enough for an adult of normal intelligence to interpret. The Chairman argued that she should attend since the Court had been cleared and was 'in every sense a private room'. 'What!' exploded Alf, turning to point at the dock, 'do you call this private?'

'That has nothing to do with it.'

'I think it has much to do with it, as father of the child.'

He strongly damned the police for bringing the case to Court — it was another example of persecution not prosecution. He thought it abominable that a Chief Constable and an Inspector, who both regularly attended church, should wish to drag a child into Court on such a charge: 'This is a blot on a child's life and I wish to lodge a strong protest against it.'

The Magistrates retired. On their return, the Chairman informed Cobb that no order would be made against his daughter, but he would be fined 2s 6d plus costs for his offence. 'It is pleasing,' responded Alf contemptuously, 'to see that such Christian men sit on the Bench.' Polly, who had been sitting at the rear of the Court, suddenly rushed forward, screaming excitedly, 'It's a great shame, it's a great shame.' She fiercely contested the fairness of the Magistrates' action and had to be physically removed by two burly police officers. The Chairman sternly rebuked Cobb for imagining there was personal 'animus' against him on the part of the police and the Chief Constable. It was pointless for him to continue to disregard the law, especially for a man of his intelligence. Alf coldly and furiously thanked him for his reference to his intelligence: 'I would pit the intelligence of my own child against the intelligence of any of the Magistrates' children, notwithstanding the smirk on your face.'

Alf Cobb left the Court that day flushed with rage and consumed with resentment. That the police should involve his child in their intimidatory tactics was the last straw; this despicable action violated all sense of natural justice. The whole affair was shot through with pure malice. He was determined not to pay the fine on principle. On Wednesday, May 10th, 1911 he was arrested and formally committed to Lewes Gaol. The following resolution was hurriedly passed by the S.D.P. branch:

> We enter our emphatic protest against the continual persecution and victimisation of our comrade, A. Cobb, by the local authorities, which has now culminated in his being arbitrarily taken to Lewes for seven days; the excuse for this unwarrantable action being the non-payment of the fine recently imposed on the trumped up charge of allowing his child to engage in street trading. In view of the fact that when the fine was imposed no alternative was offered by the Magistrates, we ask, on whose authority has our member been imprisoned and call upon the Watch Committee to at once obtain his release. It is our considered opinion that the continual harassing and persecution of our comrade is aimed at him wholly on account of his advocacy of our principles in this town. Further, we determine to spare no effort to obtain redress.

John Hutchings, a branch member, made a public complaint over the action:

> The facts, Mr Editor, are briefly as follows – Cobb's little girl came to see her 'Daddy' during the meal time allowed from school. Cobb had occasion to leave his barrow for a few minutes and the child waited for him to return. While she

was thus waiting a lady came and wished to buy some flowers. The child, anxious to help, quite innocently enough handed the flowers to the lady. For this paltry offence both the child and her father were summoned to appear before our local dispensers of justice – so called – upon the Bench. Action must needs be taken where no real offence has been committed…Truly the law is an ass. Had the politics of the individual been of a more docile type, events would, no doubt, have shaped themselves differently. I may mention that questions will be put in the House of Commons on the matter…[38]

The Hastings I.L.P. branch also protested over this 'cruel action of the so called Justices of the Peace in dragging Cobb off to jail for asking his young daughter to mind his barrow whilst he attended to one of nature's functions.'

Alf's colleagues fully expected him to discuss the implications of his imprisonment at a meeting arranged for the day of his release. To their disappointment and bewilderment he failed to appear and the meeting was abandoned. The branch membership was not aware that Alf had been released after only three days incarceration and he may have felt rather shamefaced about confronting his comrades with the news he had been freed four days earlier. He had hated the solitary confinement with nothing to occupy his mind and he had been concerned about the daily deterioration of his large stock of flowers. In prison he had learned that he could obtain an early release if he paid a part fine with certain deductions made by the Prison Governor. He had jumped at this chance to escape the mental torture of solitary confinement and returned to Hastings by rail.

He was asked to comment on his impressions of prison life, admitting it was his first experience of imprisonment:

> I should not have minded so much if I had been sentenced to hard labour – that would have given me something to do. I was hedged up in a cell in which there was barely room to stretch. From the light which entered from a window, the size of a policeman's boot, I just knew when it was day and that was all. At night a candle shining through a glass hole in the door was all the illumination I had. They fed me on gruel and water with dough and water by way of variation on another day. Am I pale? Well, I don't wonder at it.

Cobb had been allowed nothing in the way of literature apart from the Bible and a book proclaiming the virtues of soap, water and fresh air:

> This was rather ironical in a tiny, close-smelling cell where
> the sanitary arrangements were not ideal and I was expected
> to wash in three or four pints of water.

He left behind a copy of *Justice* with the Chaplain for the benefit of other prisoners.

While his Socialist colleagues waited in vain for over ninety minutes outside the Queen's Hotel to greet Cobb on his release, he was busy preparing the S.D.P's newly secured leased premises above the Electric Theatre. The branch had moved from its single room premises at 9 Priory Street because of lack of space caused by an upsurge in membership. Ten well-furnished rooms with dining and catering facilities were opened above the Wellington Place theatre in July 1911. They were to be used for business and recreational purposes and to accommodate visiting speakers. Alf told a local journalist: 'We shall always have plenty of room for people stopping here and it will be a boon to the branch to have comfortable apartments – you'll see us making great strides in the future.'

His early release disappointed many of the local Socialists who had hoped to give him a hero's welcome on his return. Their champion had stumbled and betrayed a glimpse of human frailty. One colleague observed disconsolately that it was a case of showing the white feather – he should have stuck to his guns.

Cobb soon put the prison experience behind him and his rebellious spirit remained unbroken. Shortly after regaining his freedom he was back in trouble for delivering an unlawful address on the beach opposite Denmark Place. However the Court hearing was adjourned for a month as steps were being taken to hold a town's meeting to discuss opposition to the new beach bylaw restrictions. The adjourned hearing was scheduled for June 15th to allow time for a petition requesting a public meeting to be presented to the Mayor. In Court the Acting Town Clerk read out a portion of Cobb's beach address as proof of his defiance of the Corporation and the Bench. When Alf requested another adjournment since the Mayor was out of town and unable to receive the petition, the Acting Town Clerk sprang to his feet and strongly voiced his objection. Alf put his hands on his shoulders and forced him back to his seat: 'Just sit quiet,' he advised, much to the Chairman's annoyance. He turned to the Chairman and pointed out the obvious injustice of Magistrates, who were also elected Councillors, sitting on the Bench in judgement when he was accused of breaking Corporation regulations: 'You cannot take the Town Council out of your pocket when you sit on the Bench.' He peered angrily into the Acting Town Clerk's face and told the Magistrates: 'You are being dictated to by someone who doesn't even reside in the town.'

Cobb was given no time to defend himself. Suddenly the Chairman, Alderman Weston, informed him that the Bench had decided to inflict a penalty of 20s and costs. Alf remonstrated loudly against the procedure's blatant injustice and as the Court, ignoring him, moved onto another case, he asked 'How much did you say it was?'

'Twenty shillings and costs,' replied Chief Constable James.

'I thought the Chief Constable would know.'

Alf Cobb addressing an assembly of unemployed demanding the right to work. Wellington Square, October 1910. Cobb, standing on a chair, can be seen just below the bottom right hand corner window.

CHAPTER 15

COBB'S VENDETTA

Two months after being charged with refusing to pay full fare, Alf Cobb carried out his threat of retaliation against the Hastings Tramway Company and its employees. He had witnessed the countless occasions when the trams were chock full of straphangers and dogs. Although the tramcars were designed to carry a maximum of twenty people, the Company rapidly raised these limits to permit conductors to hold thirty passengers inside and twenty dogs. These upper limits were frequently ignored by conductors.

In June 1911 Cobb summoned a Company conductor for overloading his tramcar. In a heated exchange with the Clerk to the Court he quoted bylaw after bylaw, clause after clause and section after section, placing heavy emphasis on the words 'lawful numbers' whenever they occurred. Finally the Clerk reluctantly admitted Cobb had spotted a 'curious fault in the bylaws'. Cobb, red faced and almost incoherent with anger, congratulated him on his admission: 'We Socialists always spot the faults but since the Company's solicitor also sits on the Council surely he should see to it that these faults do not exist.' The case was adjourned for a week.

When the hearing was reconvened, Cobb added two more charges against the poor conductor – for permitting passengers to travel on the platform and for standing on the top deck. Councillor Thorpe represented the Company. He alleged that the proceedings had been initiated out of personal spite rather than any motive of public interest. That a private grudge and a desire for revenge played the predominant part in the action was obviously true but cannily denied by Alf in Court. Thorpe hinted that Cobb's stand was likely to make him a public nuisance. Alf responded quietly: 'I quite understand a situation whereby one Councillor can address a set of Town Councillors on matters that have no bearing on the facts at issue.'

Thorpe asked him if he knew of any special circumstances that might have made the overcrowding necessary on the day in question.

'I know of nothing.'

'Wasn't it Empire Day?'

'But there was a parade of troops along the Front.'

'There was a parade of individuals but I did not recognise any troops.'

Alf objected to a conversation between the Clerk and Company Solicitor and was told by the Chairman: 'You get on with the case.'

'But it is impossible,' Cobb burst out, 'with this buzz of conversation. What has it to do with the Chief Constable? Why doesn't he leave off pointing out technicalities to the Clerk? I have been convicted upon enough technicalities. It is odd that honest, straightforward men cannot satisfy the Bench. But our time is coming.'

The conductor was fined the minimal sum of 1s without costs. The second and third charges were dismissed through conflicting evidence. 'Allow me to suggest,' said Alf before departing with several comrades, 'that there is always a conflict of evidence between honesty and lies.'

He left the Police Court that Thursday, June 8th, dissatisfied and in an angry and vengeful mood, determined to persevere with his vendetta against the Tramway Company. His sense of grievance was undiminished. He'd lost a day's takings and had watched the hateful Chairman impose a nominal fine – this in glaring contrast to the heavy financial penalties incurred whenever he was dragged before the Bench.

He caught a tramcar home from Queen's Road. It happened to be crowded with passengers – overcrowded. He may have deliberately waited for an overcrowded car before boarding. The one that took him homewards had three passengers standing on the running board outside and eight straphangers inside. Alf was doggedly resolute – the unfortunate conductor must face prosecution.

This time he asked the Magistrates to inflict the full penalty and order payment of costs. He solemnly informed the Chairman that a Committee had been formed to fund similar cases until the Tramway Company observed the Corporation bylaws. He insisted the overcrowding was totally unnecessary. Councillor Thorpe was again the defence counsel. He classified Cobb's prosecution as simple trumpery:

> The conductor had not appreciated Cobb was lying in wait
> by the Gas Works for any transgressor of law and order in
> the town and the keeper of every Corporation bylaw.

After the conductor had admitted the offence, it left the Bench no alternative but to fine him 5s plus costs or seven days in default.

That evening at midnight over a hundred indignant tramway employees assembled at the Company's Silverhill depot to condemn Cobb's action and rally support for their fellow workmate. The conductor was prepared to go to jail rather than pay the fine. The meeting was chaired by a Mr Brant, supported by Ryan: Cobb is going to hold a rod of terror over the conductors of this staff,' declared Brant, 'he poses as a working man's friend but gets a working man into Court. I believe that he is doing his level best to get his friends to stand on the platform so that he can successfully prosecute the conductors.

Ryan also attacked Cobb in a rousing speech. He wanted to prosecute the Company but was only prosecuting the conductors. Why was he so bitter towards the tramway employees? 'Because they had been the means of keeping him off the Council,' said Ryan. But he would discover it was the worst day's work he had ever undertaken.

The two tramway prosecutions were undoubtedly a serious political misjudgement. Cobb quickly appreciated that an attempt to gain revenge on the Company only harmed a working class individual and damaged the Socialist cause. The dispute led to a bitter controversy throughout Hastings and left a deep enmity between Cobb's supporters and the tramway employees. Several Social Democrats were so embarrassed that they helped subscribe to a fund to pay the conductor's fine.

Alf tried to justify his tactics observing that the fewer tramcars that ran, the fewer men were employed. Somehow he had gained detailed inside knowledge of the employees' working conditions. He knew of individuals who had tried to form a tramway union but instead became marked men watched by Company inspectors. How one employee was forced to go before his superiors and lost pay for daring to smile. How men were held in reserve in the depots and never received a penny unless the reserve tramcars were taken out on the road. How it was company policy to pay their employees no overtime for working extra hours; instead they could take time off whenever the management did not require their services. He maintained that such conditions turned tramway servants into Company slaves.

Cobb was well aware of the likely damage to his future electoral prospects and spiritedly told his colleagues: 'I do not care a snap of my fingers if my action affects my chances at the Borough Council elections in November.'

The following day many town centre pavements were chalked, drawing attention to the proposed open-air debate at Caroline Parade that evening between the tramway employee's champion, Ryan, and Alf Cobb of the S.D.P. In the event Ryan did not appear; he had heeded police advice about possible public disorder. Cobb was left to address the unusually large crowd that had gathered, on his own. He was subjected to a constant barrage of heckling from a section of the spectators. He repeatedly insisted that the

Tramway's solicitor had paid the conductor's fine after the Court hearing – he had witnessed the gaoler give Thorpe the correct change. This made it quite unnecessary to have a 'whip round' to pay the fine or for the conductor concerned to prepare himself for imprisonment.

The meeting ended with Alf, looking pale and unwell, wagering two sovereigns that the fine had been paid and that a certain number of cars remained in reserve in Company sheds at certain times of the day.

Correspondence began to appear in the local press complaining about the 'disgustingly disorderly meeting'. Ryan wrote to one editor:

> The employees are exceedingly sorry that the little privilege that they had given to the public in the past must now be discontinued through the action of Mr Cobb and I trust the inconvenience caused to the public will be placed on the proper shoulders.[39]

Cobb forwarded to the press a copy of the resolution that had concluded the Caroline Parade meeting, which had been carried by an overwhelming majority:

> This meeting of Hastings townspeople are of the opinion that the overloading of cars belonging to the Hastings Tramway Co. is a source of danger and a menace to the comfort of the travelling public and calls on the town authorities to immediately take steps to prevent its future occurrence. This meeting further considers the Tramway system is seriously understaffed, which entails overwork upon those employed. It therefore calls on the Company to afford a better service of cars than at present prevails and it demands a higher rate of wages than obtained today.[40]

It was generally accepted that Mugsborough's tramway employees were amongst the lowest paid in the country. Alf's accusations about constant overcrowding also had substance. This is shown in another letter published in the local press:

> The spirit of overcrowding in these cars is fast becoming a public scandal and any prosecution, persecution or even electrocution which may be awarded to the offending parties will have my supreme support.[41]

CHAPTER 16

BEN TILLETT AND THE GREAT TRANSPORT STRIKE

In August 1911 a great transport strike gripped the cities of London and Liverpool with rail, road and river transport brought virtually to a standstill. As the labour unrest spread amongst the waterside workers, London's entire dockland gradually closed down, establishing a commercial stranglehold and bringing the city's population to the brink of starvation. Ben Tillett took control of a Strike Committee located on Tower Hill and played a leading part in negotiating substantial gains for most of the port workers.

In Liverpool, Tom Mann co-ordinated the transport workers' general strike after the Port's ship owners had locked out the cargo handlers. For several days the City came under siege as the Town Hall was fired and widespread rioting became difficult to contain. Troops found it hard to restore order because of the disrupted transport network. The strike by Liverpool railwaymen encouraged other pockets of railway staff dotted across the country to stop work. By August 17th union leaders recognised the railwaymen's grievances were sufficiently strong to call a national strike. Executives of the railway unions sent out some two thousand telegrams nation-wide impelling their staff to strike at once: 'The loyalty of each means victory for all'. Two days later the railways were so badly dislocated that very few trains were running. Troops were dispatched and trains placed 'under military protection'. But the stoppage was not complete and in Hastings the national rail strike received very little support with railway workers remaining solidly loyal to their employers. Not a single railman struck at either of the two main rail stations in support of their London colleagues, although engine drivers were picketed at Victoria and Charing Cross. On the evening of August 18th, branch members of the Amalgamated Society of Railway Servants met at the Beehive Dining Rooms to adopt a circumspect 'wait and see' approach. In a matter of days the rail strike was over. Union leaders, alarmed at the violent turn of events, called the strike off and pledged assistance to a Special Commission of Inquiry.

The Hastings railway staff's loyalty was recognised by the travelling public with a fund opened to reward their reluctance to strike. W. H. Smith's station bookstall eagerly undertook to receive subscriptions. Not only did Hastings railwaymen continue working, but many were transferred to assist at other stations. Striking railwaymen elsewhere regarded this as blacklegging.

Despite this, Hastings did not escape all the effects of the rail strike. The normal passenger and goods trains were suspended and anxious holidaymakers were forced to rely on a restricted service. Bread was in short supply as London supplies of flour and grain ceased: meat supplies were generally short and petrol quickly became scarce. Local tradesmen sent their goods to country villages by carrier in preference to rail and carriers to and from Hastings enjoyed a sudden but short-lived boom.

In late August, Alf Cobb referred to the recent strike at a Socialist meeting at the Fishmarket. The events, he said, showed that Liberals were the enemies of trade unionism. The Government had used troops and police in the industrial unrest solely in the interest of railway directors. He understood that arrangements had been made to transfer local policemen to the disaffected areas. Even Corporation employees were asked to enrol as special constables. He thought it utterly unnecessary for the military to be called out during the strike and blamed the Asquith administration for the bloodshed that had resulted. As for the London press' suggestion that judges should be appointed to deal with disputes between labour and capital, ninety nine out of a hundred sat on the bench to further the interests of their own class. Instead the working class should celebrate the courage of the striking railwaymen. He urged Hastings' working men to follow their example and unite to improve their conditions.

Meanwhile the local authorities' harassment of Alf continued. He was back before the Bench in September for having his fruit barrow parked without a light. His lamp had broken and he had sent a schoolboy to replace the glass. In that intervening period, his barrow, illuminated by street lighting, had come under police observation. When Cobb asked the police witnesses in Court if they had seen any tramcars along the Front without lights the following evening the Chief Constable leapt to their aid, describing the question as irrelevant. Cobb glanced at the Chairman and told him the Bench was under the Chief Constable's thumb. Although Alf had only turned the light out because the glass was smashed he was ordered to pay a fine plus costs.

Earlier in the month he had been involved in a rowdy disruption of two

Young Liberal outdoor meetings. He joined a group of earnest young men, wearing straw hats and accompanied by well-dressed ladies, at Caroline Parade. They had surrounded a youthful speaker mounted on a small stand. The meeting was peaceful and orderly until the lecturer made an untimely reference to Socialism.

'Since the time of the first Socialist...' he began, but was cut off in mid-sentence.

'Who was the first Socialist?' demanded Cobb repeatedly, never to receive a satisfactory reply. Alf was assailed with a stream of invective and personal abuse by the hitherto passive spectators.

The second Young Liberal gathering at the Fishmarket was reduced to such scenes of disorder and riot that Cobb was charged with using language calculated to cause a breach of the peace. He was also summonsed for continuing his address after 9 p.m. He had provocatively set up his platform side by side with the Liberals. To furious jibes from the many onlookers, he lashed out at the Liberal Government's past and present legislation. One of the funnier episodes occurred after he generously offered his Socialist platform to any Young Liberal willing to expound his views. Eventually to great Liberal cheers a supporter climbed onto the stand, announced their next open meeting and swiftly disappeared into the crowd.

'Had yer on a bit of bread,' someone shouted at Cobb.

'When I ask for a Liberal opponent and this is the sort of bread they give me, I can only say it is – *stale bread*,' he sneered.

Once the Liberal meeting closed, Cobb jumped onto another box and harangued the crowd that remained. The stragglers were infuriated when he pointed out that it was their political friends that had called out the troops during the Great Strike to shoot down their fellow workers. As for the election last November in St. Clement's, it was a disgrace to the working men of the ward. At this total chaos ensued.

In his Courtroom defence Alf Cobb gave numerous examples of local bylaw infringements – the Beach Concert pavilion manager never requested written permission to hold performances after nine o'clock and permission was not given for the recent drilling of schoolchildren on the beach. After applause from Cobb's supporters was suppressed by the Bench, Alf turned around to the auditorium and said: 'This is Russia, friends. Don't make too much noise.' He was fined the equivalent of several days' earnings.

On a Wednesday evening in October, Ben Tillett returned to Hastings. Hundreds of spectators crowded into Wellington Square to hear him lecture on the contrasting conditions of life between rich and poor. His address was intended to rally support for three local members of the Social Democrats contesting seats at the next month's municipal elections. Tillett referred to the scenes of panic witnessed by the wealthy classes of the Metropolis during the dock strike. He appealed to all those present to vote for the Socialists – the workers built the town and had a right to representation on its Council.

News of Tillett's second visit to Hastings, so soon after the great London transport strike, was blacked out by the press. Cobb was later to charge the newspapers with deliberately boycotting his election campaign. Once again he stood for the Old Town Ward of St. Clements against the Liberal Councillor Felton Smith. Once more Liberals and Tories combined to sink their differences in a concerted bid to secure Smith's return. Smith turned down an invitation to debate the election issues with Cobb because of 'other engagements'. Alf accused him of being simply too frightened to stand on the same platform. He alleged there was a public conspiracy between his Liberal opponent and Councillor Morgan:

> Felton Smith stroked Morgan's back last year – this year it's Morgan's turn to stroke his back. As for Smith, he had done nothing to help the town's working classes outside offering his services to a free school breakfast canteen where he had stood at one side rubbing his hands and never budging an inch until some plates were thrust into his hand and he was made to help.

'Some people might think I'm just being personal,' Cobb said to his onlookers' amusement, 'but that merely means I'm telling the truth; when I get to the Council, I shall be just as bluff, just as blunt and just as abrupt as I am now'.

Sadly all three Socialist candidates were badly beaten. Cobb lost considerable ground in the Old Town where Smith polled nearly 350 more votes. His heavy defeat became the talking point of the 1911 November elections.

Several factors contributed to his poor showing, not least the misguided and politically suicidal prosecution of the tramway conductors. The Socialists attributed their defeat to a mistake in promoting a number of candidates instead of concentrating their efforts on one ward. Tom King, who polled only 97 votes in Silverhill, announced his intention of issuing writs for slander against members of the Liberal Committee at Hollington;

so misrepresentation again played a part in the outcome.

After the results were declared Cobb gave an impromptu open-air speech. He reminded his audience to remember at the next parliamentary election how the two main parties had united in their statement that there were no policy differences between them. He said despondently:

> It wasn't only their united front that had brought the Socialist defeat, but the Roman Catholic priest, the Protestant parson, the publican and the slum property owner who have worked hand in hand to keep members of the working class off the Council. The whole election simply means that working men are perfectly satisfied with the mismanagement of their town's affairs.

An open–air meeting of the SDF, on the beach near the Queen's Hotel.

CHAPTER 17

THE LIBEL CASE

In September 1910 Hastings Town Council ordered its sanitary officer to take samples of butter from local tradesmen for analysis. The analyst was later to report unfavourably on four of the samples. One of these came from Atkins Bros and Cox of London Road, St. Leonards. George Cox was the director of this catering business. He was also a member of the Council. The names of the tradesmen involved were quickly suppressed. The analyst's findings were not publicly disclosed until after the Sanitary Committee reported back to the Council. The Committee recommended the Corporation not to institute proceedings on this occasion even though the sale of adulterated foodstuffs clearly contravened the law.

On the 21st October, Councillor Warner put a series of questions to the Sub-Committee Chairman. Had the Committee been influenced in its decision by any consideration that one of the vendors selling adulterated samples was a Council member? If not, why were all the prosecutions abandoned?

During the 1910 November Council election campaign, two thousand copies of a specially prepared election edition of *Justice* flooded the Hastings streets. The individual responsible for the local edition was Alf Cobb. Councillor Cox was infuriated by an article written by two other members of the S.D.P. branch entitled 'The Corrupt State of Hastings Public Affairs'. The following passage caused the gravest offence:

> Just recently the Council tried their hand in connection with the Food and Drugs Act; they sent out for samples of butter. The people's food must be looked after, you know. Samples were obtained. We are informed one came from a very prominent Councillor's establishment, and was found to contain nearly 50% of margarine! The Council's efforts in this direction are now suspended. They dare not proceed against one of themselves. The sacred fetish of Hastings Councillorship must be protected. Moreover did they proceed in the matter, the Councillor in question from a business point of view would suffer. Business is probably

bad with him, more of his trade might go to other shops; so
he is safe at present.

The article served to deepen the bitter personal feud that had existed
for years between George Cox and Alf Cobb. Cox's solicitors wrote to
Cobb in March 1911, asking for an apology or they would initiate libel
proceedings. The solicitors related how their client had suffered the
indignity of people calling after him in the streets 'Margarine' or 'bad butter
Cox'. Alf admitted that he was entirely responsible for the publication but
denied any libel since Cox's name was never mentioned. *Justice*'s own
solicitors also denied there were any grounds for libel.

After Cobb had refused to submit an apology, Cox pushed ahead with
the threatened libel suit. Five months were to elapse before the case was
brought before the High Court because Cox was undecided about also
prosecuting the wholesale supplier of the adulterated butter. He refused to
bring the libel action before a Sussex Jury fearing perhaps that some of the
jurors may have had Hastings connections.

Justice Darling presided over a Special Jury in the King's Bench
Division of the High Court. Alf was quite prepared to defend himself in
Court but others were involved in the action, including Harry Quelch,
London editor of *Justice*, together with the proprietor, W. A. Woodroffe and
Twentieth Century Press Ltd., the company responsible for the journal's
national publication. The publishing company appointed a barrister and
legal assistant for the defence, advising Alf not to give evidence from the
witness box.

Cox's Counsel argued that the Hastings firm had purchased the butter
in perfect good faith from a wholesaler in Wellington Place, quite innocent
of any knowledge that the product was unsound. The article in *Justice*
inferred that Hastings Councillors had been corrupted by their refusal to
prosecute in order to save Cox's position in public affairs. The article's
publication had seriously injured his client's public and private reputation
and lost him many customers. It was absurd humbug for Cobb to suggest
that because nobody's name was mentioned 'where did the libel come in?'
The plaintiff's barrister hammered this point home relentlessly. Finally the
Judge intervened testily acknowledging the Bench's appreciation that it was
not necessary to print a man's name to incur libel.

Cox gave evidence; he had suffered considerable annoyance ever since
the article came out: 'Twelve months ago, I remember distinctly that Mr.
Cobb was passing in the streets with Polly Bassett when I was talking to

two gentlemen, when he called out "margarine and flowers in the Park".' Justice Darling, ignorant of the earlier Parks and Gardens scandal, displayed a sense of humour he was to show throughout the hearing. He looked at the wrapper round the butter exhibit and exclaimed: 'Ah, I see that this is called "meadowsweet" butter!'

A. R. McCall defended. He made a special reference to the Parks and Gardens Investigation Committee's report recommending the resignation of officials without censuring any Councillors and the Sanitary Committee's resolution not to prosecute certain cases under the Food and Drugs Act. He asked Cox if he was present when Alderman Hutchings stated that one cause of the town's decline was that its Town Council was a mass of corruption.

'Were you present in Council when Councillor Morgan asked if any member had been in receipt of flowers from the public gardens?'

'Yes.'

'Did anybody present give any detail?'

'Nobody gave any detail,' admitted Cox uncomfortably.

McCall's strenuous defence that the passage in question was fair comment was not accepted. The jury returned after only a few minutes upholding the libel. The defendants were fined a total of £200 damages with costs.

The outcome of the libel action caused repercussions far beyond the confines of Mugsborough. George Cox struggled desperately to recover his costs from any assets held by the defendants. He lost this financial battle. Twentieth Century Press, rather than pay out, simply placed their business in the hands of a receiver, thereby safeguarding the interests of its debenture holders. Cox might have petitioned for a receiving order against Cobb but Alf calmly underwent his public examination that assessed his assets as 'nil'. Harry Quelch quit as Editor of *Justice* and filed a petition for bankruptcy to forestall any attempts to exact damages. Woodroffe was later ordered to pay Cox at the rate of 12s a month. Cox never received a penny.

In April 1912 a notification of the receiving order against Cobb was placed in the *London Gazette*. The Bankruptcy Hearing was held on April 23rd. Alf explained that he was a member of the Hastings Social Democratic Party, now known as the British Socialist Party. He was branch treasurer (earlier in 1912 Frederick Fermor replaced Cobb as Secretary). Cobb's address was given as 226 Old London Road, Ore. He stated in court that he earned his living as a hawker — it was Miss Bassett who used part of the premises for her greengrocer's shop. He was Miss Bassett's tenant.

Since she claimed the contents of the shop and all the furniture in the house, he was unable to declare any assets. As for his annual profits as a hawker, these amounted to £80 – the exact amount needing for living expenses for himself and one child.

'Haven't you kept any kind of books?'

'No; they were unnecessary.'

'Yours is just a cash trade?'

'Yes.'

He was asked about the local branch's account with the London and Westminster Bank.

'There is only a small balance,' Cobb replied.

'Fourpence, I think,' informed the Official Receiver.

'Was there a larger balance at the date of the receiving order?'

'I can't say; I think not,' responded Alf.

Councillor George Cox grew increasingly irritated. Four days after Cobb's 'fruitless' bankruptcy hearing, he brought a judgement summons against Quelch and Woodroffe in a further attempt to obtain the £200 damages and £209 Court costs. Quelch told the Justice he was in no position to make an offer; his salary of £4 a week was entirely dependent on his position as editor, but the Company was now in liquidation. Woodroffe described himself as a printer and argued it was absolute nonsense for him to be involved: 'they might just as well have got judgement against the errand boy for I can't offer anything.'

Quelch was ordered to pay 30s a month and Woodroffe 20s. Cox got nothing. The Court Order cost George Cox an additional £50 to his mounting libel expenses. He did succeed in forcing the compulsory winding up of Twentieth Century Press:

> Not satisfied with this he has pursued the editor and manager with a view to compelling them to pay what he has been unable to realise from the Company. He appears to imagine that conduct of a socialist propaganda organ is as lucrative as that of catering for holiday makers in a fashionable watering place. He is mistaken. Socialist agitation does not pay, in a Liberal bourgeois sense, nor sufficiently to enable two of its poorer apostles to put up a sum of £400 when called upon to do so![42]

The Court judgement was completely ignored by both Quelch and Woodroffe. Three weeks later the Hastings Establishment started practical steps to dig their Council colleague out of his financial hole. Somehow the local Socialists obtained access to a secret communication from the Mayor seeking to raise funds to offset George Cox's loss. The letter, headed private and confidential, was passed on to *Justice* and published with minimal comment:

> *Concerning ourselves* – the following has come into our hands. It may be interesting to our readers as evidence of the solidarity and vindictiveness of the bourgeoisie when in pursuit of their prey.

> The Mayor's Parlour,
> Town Hall,
> Hastings, 16th May 1912.

> Dear Sir,

> Cox V. Twentieth Century Press and others.
> May I bring to your notice the particulars of this case? Councillor George Cox was for a long time subjected to considerable annoyance from a local leader of the Socialist Party; this annoyance eventually culminated in the publication in *Justice* of 29th October, 1910 of the very serious and injurious article which formed the ground of the recent libel action referred to above, I do not think therefore it will be necessary to remind you that the libellous article contained in *Justice* not only reflected on Mr Cox's personal character and business reputation but also imputed dishonourable conduct to him and other members of the Town Council in the discharge of their public duties.
> Mr Cox has availed himself of all means of enforcing the judgement against the defendants, Twentieth Century Press Ltd., Alfred J. Cobb, Harry Quelch and Woodroffe but without any pecuniary result. The Twentieth Century Press Limited are being wound up compulsorily by the Court but the debenture holders are in possession of the assets by means of a receiver. Mr Cobb has been made bankrupt and though the other two defendants are under order of Court to pay the small sums of 30s and 20s monthly, nothing so far has been received from them.
> The plaintiff's costs in the action were taxed at £209.14s and he has since incurred further expenses in prosecuting his Judgement amounting to over £50.
> Under these unfortunate circumstances and having regards to the fact that Councillor Cox was considerably influenced by Public and Commercial interests in prosecuting his action against the parties in question, I, together with several prominent members of the Council and Fellow Townsmen, feel that the Plaintiff ought not to be

called upon to bear the whole cost of the proceedings.

Knowing that Mr Cox has always taken an earnest and active part in local trade and public matters, I feel that there must be many of his fellow townsmen and others who would like to join in our efforts in the direction I have indicated and who will agree that the present is an excellent opportunity to shew appreciation of services freely given in the interests of the Town and Trade. I have only to add that I am willing and shall be pleased to receive subscriptions towards the fund which is being raised and these may be addressed to me at the Town Hall and will be greatly acknowledged.

I am dear sir,
Yours faithfully,
Geo. Hutchings,
Mayor.

In August 1912 Cox's London solicitors obtained a committal order against Harry Quelch from the High Court. The solicitors wrote to Quelch informing him that a committal order had been drawn up for six weeks. After August 27th it would become enforceable. Quelch printed the solicitors' letter in *Justice* with the following note:

I am grateful to the many comrades and friends who have written expressing sympathy and offering suggestions. As I am unable to pay Mr Cox and have no desire to accept six weeks imprisonment his solicitors here so kindly offer me as an alternative, I am filing a petition for bankruptcy. I could not reasonably appeal to my comrades to pay the debt. They have already too many calls upon them.

It must not be forgotten, also that the same judgement to which I fell victim resulted in the winding up of the T.C.P.; and all good comrades will surely wish to do all in their power to set our press on its feet again.[43]

Quelch resigned as *Justice*'s Editor before his public examination in the London Bankruptcy Court on October 18th – a position he had held since 1892. At the hearing his failure was attributed directly to the libel action. His liability was confined entirely to the damage and costs inflicted by Cox's legal manoeuvres – his assets estimated at 7s 8d, held in a bank account.

In September, *Justice* began the reorganisation of its press. The journal announced it would shortly issue one-shilling shares and earnestly appealed to its readership to take up as many as possible: 'we want to make *Justice* the property as well as the expression of the principles and policy of the

Party.'[44]

On November 16th, the paper informed its readers that 'we have succeeded in raising by subscriptions for shares and loans the amount of money necessary for the purchase of our press from the Debenture Holders and the launching of the new company.'

Quelch was reinstated on a reduced salary of £3 a week. In July 1913 he was granted a suspended discharge from bankruptcy.

Polly & Alf's greengrocery shop at 226 Old London Road, Ore.
(The street numbers have since been altered.)

CHAPTER 18

HASTINGS AND THE GREAT WAR

Despite the local election setbacks the Socialist branch membership continued to grow right up to the outbreak of the Great War. Open-air addresses proceeded throughout the summer of 1911 although overshadowed by the libel case and the Tramway Company affair.

Harry Quelch had paid a second visit to Hastings in April. In September 1911 Jack Williams gave two autobiographical lectures covering his thirty years as a Socialist agitator. Williams was an old and greatly admired friend of Hyndman. He had preached the socialist cause from the dock gates during the Great Dock Strike of 1889 alongside Ben Tillett, Will Thorne and others. He took a prominent part in the West End Riots of 1886 after the collapse of sugar refineries had cast large numbers out of work in the East End of London. His involvement in the Riots led to his trial for sedition and later acquittal at the Old Bailey. Hyndman described him as an 'indefatigable figure'.

Cobb spent part of the summer outside Hastings giving a series of 'excellent' outdoor lectures in Tunbridge Wells for the town's Socialist branch. He attended the London National Executive meetings of the S.D.P. in November that were to re-style the movement as the British Socialist Party. The Hastings branch held meetings regularly at the Electric Palace in Wellington Place during the winter of 1911-12.

By the summer of 1912 a resumption of Anti-Socialist propaganda was in full swing. The Season also witnessed the opening campaign of the Hastings branch of the Tariff Reform League – a campaign that did not escape the attention of the Socialists, with lively scenes at the Fishmarket. In the autumn Tom King again lost heavily in the Silverhill Ward; Cobb's bankruptcy barred him from standing.

Alf issued the following invitation for outside speakers, published in the London edition of *Justice* in April 1912:

> Hastings air is bracing and excellent for the lungs as one can see by the numerous homes for consumptives with their wide-open windows in this neighbourhood. But why wait for consumption to claim you a victim? If you are a speaker, come to Hastings for your holidays and exercise your lungs

on the Socialist platform thus benefiting your health as well as the cause.

Surely a novel way to advertise the charms of a seaside resort.

The year 1913 was uneventful. Alf was engaged in a minor scuffle with the landlord of the Queen's Hotel Saloon in September. The landlord, Percy Gourlay, had called Cobb a 'low-down cur' and a 'dirty Socialist', catching hold of his sleeve. He declined to serve Cobb a drink and asked him to leave alleging that he had created disturbances in every public house in Hastings. Since Gourlay later refused to apologise Cobb summoned him for assault. The landlord's wife gave evidence that her husband had stopped two men 'who looked like giving Mr Cobb a good hiding'. Alf had been squirted with a water pistol after insulting several saloon customers. At that juncture the case was halted and dismissed.

In the last days of December 1913 Lord Roberts, President of the National Service League, wrote to the Hastings press outlining his proposals for strengthening the Territorial Army. His proposal that military training should be made compulsory for all youths was scathingly dismissed by a local correspondent, Albert Rulf: 'Our boys would be better employed mastering Esperanto or German languages, swimming, rowing, etc. than in learning how to kill some probable invader'. His attitude made no sense to Alf Cobb. He thought that although Lord Roberts' ideas on compulsory universal training diverged from a democratically based National Citizen Army, nevertheless it was a start in securing a first line of defence and might help significantly to reduce naval expenditure. He observed that:

> The spirit of greed, not brotherhood, prevails. England is still a commercial nation; its people have not yet accepted the principles of Socialism. For the sake of our population, even the markets must be obtained; this must continue until the people exercise their intelligence. Hence the Navy is necessary; the Army also necessary and more than ever necessary is the establishment of a National Citizen Army. Our lads are put to much worse tasks than receiving military training: let this be undertaken not in their own time, but during the time many of them would be engaged in less congenial occupation for their masters ...[45]

Cobb was attacked for these 'militaristic' remarks and called Lord Roberts' Socialist henchman. A critic named Thomas Upfield wrote to the *Hastings Observer* insisting that only a few British Socialist Party members, including Will Thorne, advocated a Citizen Army; the great majority were fiercely opposed to it. (Upfield would have been correct if he had argued that a majority of the B.S.P. were uncompromisingly anti-war; the Party later split into pro and anti-war factions with Hyndman and Robert Blatchford strongly in favour). Almost overnight Blatchford's *Clarion* became aggressively militaristic, producing an equally dramatic slump in circulation. Hyndman's pro-war posturing soon caused him to be ejected from leadership of the B.S.P.

Alf Cobb denied he had ever used a single argument in favour of militarism. He maintained that training a Citizen Army did not imply service – mobilisation only occurred in the event of actual invasion. On the contrary, he argued, national defence was the exact opposite of militarism; its civilian members would not be used for wars of aggression. He insisted that the establishment of a Citizen Army had always appeared in both S.D.F. and S.D.P. programmes at their annual conferences. Upfield was just trying to prove he was a Socialist renegade. Cobb sought to justify his stance publicly:

> Your correspondent scoffs at the possibility of war... soldiering, I presume in your opinion, is unworthy of the age in which we live. Have you forgotten the Boer War? The use of soldiering in Belfast. Dublin, Leith, Swansea and elsewhere by the present Government, who allowed soldiers to shoot down unarmed men, women and children! Have you no recollection of the English troops shooting down Englishmen in Johannesburg last July? That the present Government sanctioned this unholy murder? Wherever have you been Mr Upfield? Are you really alive? Are you only dense? Why the age is an age of militarism...
>
> There is always a possibility of war, until there is a universal agreement among civilised people to disarm. Much to the regret of your correspondent and myself that time is not yet. What are we to do in the meantime? We must consider how best we can transform our present Army and Navy without endangering the welfare of our people. The first step towards disarmament is to arm the people. Every man a citizen. Every citizen a soldier. The people to decide between peace and war.[46]

By early 1914 Cobb realised that war was inevitable and that the country was wholly unprepared. In August the Mayor addressed the Hastings townspeople, exhorting them to stand side by side, shoulder to shoulder and 'share and share alike, whatever crisis arises'. He condemned the action of wealthy hoarders of foodstuffs whose bulk purchases pushed up prices and hit the 'poorer brethren placed on the lowest spoke of fortune's wheel.' Socialist sentiments were suddenly fashionable amongst some of the Hastings luminaries!

When war came the Drill Hall in Middle Street was rapidly opened to encourage recruitment; men were pressed to enrol to meet the quota set for Hastings. Lord Kitchener had requested 100,000 volunteers. Relief Committees were established to alleviate wartime distress. Alf Cobb appreciated that many local residents would find such charity degrading and insulting. He understood that many working class breadwinners would be 'placed where the battle is fiercest'; many would never return:

> The people's needs are left at the mercy of kind hearted, generously disposed persons and their relief committees. The people are responding to their country's needs with their fathers, brothers and sons. The people, then, are deserving of more than relief.
> Let the Government, then, immediately undertake the control and supply of the means of life for the people...
> Let the Government also make the hoarding of foods, etc., a crime. It is not relief the people should receive, but justice.[47]

Several stirring appeals were made in Wellington Square in support of recruitment into the Regular Army. Mayor Hocking, Lord Hythe, Coulson Kernahan and Lieut. Colonel Whittle, the Recruiting Officer, headed the enrolment drive. The Mayor stated that he was proud that throughout the Empire and in 'good old Hastings' the call had been made and was being nobly answered. He felt sure that the grand patriotic spirit which had inspired their fathers would still inspire the men of Hastings. But the 'grand patriotic spirit' was not so easily rekindled. After three week's hard endeavour by Whittle and his helpers, based at an office in Brook Street, less than two hundred had been enlisted. Two Hundred! The *Hastings Observer* was appalled at the poor response:

> Think of it, Hastings – with its thousands of young men, hundreds of them leading an aimless life – unable to do more than send a beggarly two hundred to help King and Country in a time of vital trial.[48]

Lieut. Colonel Whittle was downcast. He expressed his keen disappointment 'considering the population of Hastings and the fact that the people here may be said to be almost within earshot of the actual hostilities, I had every reason to expect something better.' Whittle's appeal had an infinitely better response from the surrounding country districts. Even Alf Cobb was surprised at the poor Hastings response, particularly after learning that the majority of the volunteers came from outside the borough. He wrote:

> Lieut. Colonel Whittle is a glutton for his toil, but the recruiting barometer registers little above zero. Something is wrong. What is it? Employers and other wealthy folk are using all manner of artifices and threats to get recruits. Men who have families are reluctant to join. Who is to look after the wives and children? Wives of men who were called up nearly a month ago have not been paid. A working woman cannot get credit; the butcher, the grocer, etc., with whom she trades cannot afford to trust. The Moratorium does not extend to her. Married men are prepared to go to the Front if adequate provision is made for those left behind. And why not?
>
> The so-called voluntary system has failed mainly because of the niggardly policy adopted towards our soldiers. To appeal to the women to shun those who remain is equally inept and unfair; in the main the women want their men here, not probably maimed for life or killed upon a European battlefield. The women, as well as men, are called upon to suffer.[49]

Alf Cobb, then aged forty, volunteered before the year was out. He spent three and a half years in active service enlisted in a Labour Battalion in France. He married Polly Bassett so that she could receive his army pay. One night in 1918 during battle he fell down a steep railway embankment injuring his head as he landed heavily on the track. This fall was to be the cause of his premature death in 1921. After his army discharge he became prone to recurrent epileptic fits and never recovered his full health.

The first public announcement of Alf's return to Hastings is found in a short article in the local press, dated December 14th, 1918:

> Cobb bobs up at a meeting of the Coalition candidate Laurence Lyon at Middle Street Drill Hall last Wednesday night. His question to the candidate showed that his active service has not shaken his old beliefs. One bone of contention appeared to be the difference between demobilisation and discharge. The heckling was good humoured.[50]

Lyon, who later became the Hastings Member of Parliament, promised Cobb a private interview.

CHAPTER 19

CELEBRATING PEACE WITHOUT PLENTY

Once the Armistice had been signed on November 11th, 1918, a spontaneous desire to celebrate the troops' homecoming engulfed Mugsborough's company of rejoicing civilian dignitaries. A special town's meeting was called, in April 1919, to assess the most appropriate means of celebrating peace. The Mayor's Welcome Home Committee laid plans for a fancy civic reception and grand banquet. The official celebrations were to include, on a designated day in July, a procession of decorated motor cars, carriages and prams in Alexandra Park and an evening carnival along the seafront.

But the Mayor had badly misread the mood of the discharged and demobbed servicemen. Strong feelings soon surfaced among the men against such extravagance. They regarded the proposed Welcome Home festivities as a sheer waste of money, particularly when the widows of those fallen in battle had children to clothe and feed. The Mayor was humbled and embarrassed. How should the money collected for the planned entertainment be spent? He hurriedly set up another meeting to sound out the men's views. Ex-servicemen jammed the Sessions Court hearing. The Mayor's original idea of a grand fete and illuminated address was immediately and unceremoniously ditched. A resolution that the money raised should be used for the benefit of deserving widows and children was unopposed. Alf Cobb was the main representative for the men's views and little time passed before an exasperated Mayor asked him not to interrupt.

'I am not here to be dictated to even by the Mayor of Hastings,' he replied to dissent and applause. He moved an amendment that the money should be placed in the hands of the men for their own administration. An unidentified local Socialist told the Mayor they were sick and tired of flag waving and smacks on the back; the Council should put forward schemes to find men employment.

Cobb grew increasingly annoyed by the dominating manner of the platform members of the Welcome Home Fund Committee. 'This is a meeting of men returned from the War. Where are the service badges of those sitting on the Bench?' he asked pointedly.

He turned his criticism on the 'Comrades' who, in his opinion, had been foisted on the discharged men by the Government: 'People have discovered that the right association is an association run by the men themselves'. Cobb had correctly judged the attitude of the men. His resolution was unanimously adopted. It read as follows:

> That this meeting of ex-servicemen keenly appreciate the efforts of the people of Hastings to provide a Welcome Home for them, but owing to the present inadequate pensions and allowances granted to the widows and dependants of our fallen comrades and others who die after discharge, and the non-existence of a fund to meet immediate distress in these cases, feel that the money collected should be placed in the hands of two trustees and a Committee appointed from the discharged and demobilised men in the town to form a Fund for this purpose.

The proposal was the final humiliation for Mayor Hocking.

Alf Cobb's low regard for the right wing, officer-controlled 'Comrades of the Great War' was not enhanced when their Hastings branch decided to encourage the employment of two non-union staff engaged by the local Gas Company. This gesture infuriated other unionised gas employees and precipitated a strike with demands for improved pay and conditions. Cobb was voted onto the Committee of the National Federation of Discharged and Demobilised Soldiers and Sailors. The Federation took a completely opposite line to the 'Comrades' in its backing for the striking Hastings gas workers.

At a general meeting of the 'Comrades', Colonel Cafe warned that Mr Cobb was 'out to stir bad blood between ourselves and the Soldiers' and Sailors' Federation'. The meeting should seek a public apology from him. Another member, Captain Appleby, also made reference to Alf's accusation that the Association had been thrust on ex-servicemen by the Government: 'I wish it were so; I wish that the Government realised that we are the only guard against Bolshevism in this country.'

Several factors had conspired to persuade the Captain that the Bolshevik 'contagion' had crossed the Channel on board troop ships homeward bound. In June 1917 an anti-war Soviet convention had been organised by Socialists in Leeds. The convention warmly endorsed a resolution calling for Workers' and Soldiers' Councils in Britain. Reports of troops forming Soldiers' Councils in Egypt were later confirmed. Earlier that year, in January 1919, ten thousand troops had mutinied at Folkestone, and Dover experienced a similar outbreak of mutiny but on a smaller scale. Disaffection, insubordination and open resistance to discipline spread to many other army camps. Lorry loads of angry mutineers drove into Whitehall demanding interviews with Government officials.

Partial demobilisation had begun on December 9th 1918, one month after the Armistice was signed. The problem of absorbing discharged servicemen back into civilian employment deeply concerned Lloyd George. His advisers devised a strategy to stagger demobilisation and thereby blunt the mass impact of post-war unemployment. But the scheme did not embody any state subsidisation or public work projects. Many found work in the industrial areas without difficulty. But Hastings had no industry worth mentioning, outside fishing. By January 1920 a thousand ex-servicemen were among the 1600 registered unemployed. Hopes of the construction of a new world vanished in Mugsborough. Disillusionment and despair set in. The spirit of the trenches seemed far removed.

Alf Cobb was on the Hastings Employment Committee that requested information from the Ministry of Labour about possible Government grants to aid new local industries. Back came the standard response – private enterprise must be relied upon to reduce unemployment: the Government was not prepared to allocate public resources to assist private employment schemes. Peacetime Hastings of course did not fit in with this non-interventionist approach.

The Employment Committee arranged a meeting with Laurence Lyon, coalition candidate for Hastings, in April 1918. The question of state subsidies was top of the agenda. Alf Cobb reminded Lyon that two years before he had assured them of a Government promise to provide the finance necessary to re-employ the ex-troops. Lyon refuted this – the Government might have pledged to 'look after the men in the way it thought fit' but he had never indicated it would subsidise industry. The old soldier's cry that 'promises are not piecrust' sprang to Cobb's mind. Trench warfare was no passport into civilian occupation. Many of the town's young soldiers had never had an opportunity to learn a trade; others volunteered on the understanding that they would be able to return to their former employer – only to find the post had been filled. The disabled were employed by Hastings Corporation cleaning public lavatories or given other light work. A large number of unskilled men remained unemployed. A sense of bitterness and betrayal pervaded the Borough.

In a desperate effort to contain the swelling numbers of unemployed, a concerted bid was made to secure the construction of a local brick and glass factory. Cobb was at the centre of this local initiative. Inquiries had revealed that a suitable amount of sand deposits existed on the Sayer-Milward Estate at Fairlight to warrant the construction of a large glass factory. The owners of the Estate were contacted. Would they sell a specified acreage for the erection of a factory and workmen's dwellings? If not could the sand be purchased for delivery by rail to Doleham Halt or Hastings railway station?

Alf Cobb was sceptical about Laurence Lyon's commitment to the scheme. He simply failed, in Alf's view, to comprehend the duties and potential of his public office. For his part, Lyon insisted that a brick and glass industry was of insufficient national importance to have any chance of gaining Government aid. A subsidised glass works would compete directly with similar industries established with private finance. The Government made a clear distinction between the development of new industries, such as sugar beet, and those already well established. A week later, Alf Cobb responded to Lyon's considered judgement. He accused him of putting 'a damper on the idea'. As for his knowledge of subsidies it covered only those 'which may form a good picking for financial princes'. His challenge to meet Lyon, anytime, anywhere, to debate the issue was ignored.

The whole matter was raised again at a Town Hall meeting in June 1920. A letter was read out from Lyon stating that he was unable to attend as Parliament was sitting, but he had nothing to add to his earlier opinions. The meeting went on to discuss the idea of another interview with the Ministry of Labour. Councillor Gray advised that, this time, the word 'subsidy' should not be used. They must emphasise rather the principle of substituting employment and wages for the payment of dole. A resolution was passed along the lines he suggested and the Ministry was asked to receive a deputation from the conference. It would consist of three members from the Pensions Committee and three from the Employment Committee. Alf Cobb was one of the appointed members. But the usual muddle and mismanagement was never far away. The organisation of the deputation was a shambles. Although the Chairman of the Employment Committee was nominated, he refused to attend. He did not consider he possessed the necessary back up data and anyway thought the scheme impractical. His replacement, Alderman Fellows, also refused to attend for 'business reasons'. Colonel Langham was hastily drafted in, but was absent from the crucial preliminary tactical discussion. Thus Langham put the wrong case to the Ministry. He forgot Councillor Gray's advice and appealed for a subsidy for private ownership when the deputation had decided to apply for a Municipal grant.

The Board of Trade letter in reply made depressing reading. It categorically denied the claim that the Ministry of Munitions had ever contemplated the promotion of a glass making industry in Hastings during the war. Their investigation had looked only at the glass sand deposits to be found at Bulverhythe and south of Fairlight Church. Even so, the potential productive capacity of optical glass factories already exceeded the combined requirements of both the domestic and export trade. Such a skilled and highly technical branch of glass making would not begin to reduce the unskilled numbers of unemployed. Aside from that, H.M. Government was not rendering financial assistance to any section of the glass industry – the matter was one for private enterprise only. The Board suggested, as an alternative, that steps might be taken to lower unemployment by supplying other glass manufacturers with sand from the deposits around Hastings. Later inquiries showed that even this was not a paying proposition.

As for the creation of a Hastings brick industry – it proved a non-starter. The brickfields of Tunbridge Wells, Tonbridge, Crowborough and Bexhill easily met all Hastings' needs and the cost of transporting bricks outside the Borough boundaries was prohibitive.

Mugsborough was back to square one.

7, Brook Street. Alf Cobb's home from 1917 until his death in 1921.

CHAPTER 20

THE POST-WAR PERIOD

Hastings increasingly came to resemble an economic wasteland in the aftermath of the Great War. Its ex-servicemen cast around for any means of scraping a living to escape the lengthening dole queues. Past promises of a post-war reconstruction programme and a land fit for heroes were dismissed as empty phrases or deception by the governing class. Since the Government would not intervene on their behalf, self-reliance was the only answer. The street barrow trade revived strongly much to the consternation of shopkeepers situated near the Memorial. A large proportion of the hawkers were ex-soldiers. Soon petitions protesting against the hawkers being allowed to pitch their barrows in central thoroughfares began to reach the Town Hall. One shopkeeper complained bitterly that the present street trading irregularities gave the main streets and parade the appearance of an open-air market. Complaints were also levelled at the numerous fish stalls in King's Road, St. Leonards.

Alf Cobb led a hawkers' deputation in May 1920. He addressed the Town Council at some length. He had noticed that many petitioners often broke the bylaws with impunity but were not so closely watched by the police as the 'lower orders'. He knew that several petitioners had signed the same petition more than once making their protest 'more of a shadow than a substance'. Government Departments recognised the hawkers' case and gave grants towards the purchase of barrows, weights and scales. He feared the hawkers would not get a fair deal from the Council 'as many of them are traders bent on defending their friends'. The Mayor thanked the Deputation for its attendance but thought Mr Cobb had 'laid it on pretty thick'.

Alf had not expected any help from the Councillors but, after the Deputation withdrew, a motion was carried requesting that a Special Committee be formed to investigate alternative sites for the hawkers' barrows. Even the Mayor appreciated that many of the barrow boys were ex-servicemen and the Council should tread warily.

The summer of 1920 passed free of prosecutions but this peaceful interlude was broken with a vengeance in October. Thirteen hawkers were charged with obstructing Queen's Road on one day in September. The authorities were forced to take action because the obstruction was blatant. Rows and rows of barrows were lined up so closely together that there was less than two feet between them. Motor-cars were forced to park in the middle of the road. Alf Cobb's daughter, Florrie, then aged twenty, was one of the thirteen defendants. She spoke out sharply in her defence:

> It's a pity that a girl like myself, who has a father who cannot work, should be brought before the Bench. Is this what you call liberty and justice?

Her father's poor health prevented him from working the streets and Polly and Florrie took turns with his barrow. Another hawker told the Magistrates: 'We fought for freedom while Germany makes proper provision for its hawkers.'

The Chairman was sympathetic. He recognised that the street traders had no suitable place to stand their barrows and appreciated the Corporation was trying to resolve the situation. All the cases were adjourned 'sine die'. Later that evening the hawkers arranged a meeting to consider their response to the Council's proposal that a market site should be provided in Queen's Road for their needs. They decided to accept this offer with certain reservations. Alf Cobb suggested that they form a Costers' Union. He was elected Chairman. He ruled that in future any further fines for obstruction would be paid out of Union funds so long as the member kept within the terms of the Council agreement. Twenty hawkers joined the newly formed Union that night.

Several days after the formation of the Costermongers' Union, Alf Cobb announced, health permitting, his intention to contest the forthcoming November Municipal elections. Once again he would fight Councillor Morgan's St. Clement's Ward. But this time he ran as the nominee of the Soldiers' and Sailors' National Federation. The ex-servicemen were a powerful lobby and the Representation of the People Act vastly expanded the local government franchise. They trusted Alf and admired his dedicated work defending their interests regardless of his declining health. He easily defeated Morgan by a majority of 233, gaining 725 votes. His victory was not unexpected. His old campaigning slogan 'many are called – but few get up' had been fully realised. Cobb was unaware that death was only a matter of months away.

Alf took his place in the Council Chambers four days after the result was declared. The impact was immediate. He demanded to know what was being done to combat unemployment before the ensuing winter season. He was told that no special provision had been made in the Council's estimates for that current year. He asked if any progress had been reported by the Special Committee on Street Trading. No – the Committee business had been delayed by the local elections; the Council was awaiting a further bulletin. After heated debate, Cobb's motion that a special Sub-Committee be formed to tackle the town's unemployment was carried. As for the recommended £300 annual remuneration for the Mayor – no, he did not support its adoption. He had no intention of taking part in the Mayor's luncheon and handed in his invitation card.

Polly Bassett's niece, Annie Gannon, has lived in California for many years. Annie is the sister of 'Lizzie' Rich, a member of a well-known Old Town family. She has a vivid memory of Alf sitting in the corner of the Town Hall. He was told that if he took his seat they could start serving dinner.

'I am not hungry,' he replied, 'but you go ahead and enjoy it, while outside the unemployment office stands a crowd of men who could feed their families with what you leave and throw away.'

She remembers him returning home sickened and disgusted.

The Chairman of the new Unemployment Sub-Committee was George Cox, Alf's old enemy and initiator of the libel proceedings against him. Cox pushed forward a scheme for the construction of a new arterial road linking Sedlescombe Road North with Upper St. Helen's Road. He thought the building of the new road would open up the 'desirable' parts of the Borough for building purposes.

The Government sanctioned the construction, promising a grant towards half the cost. Cox's scheme received Council approval in December, 1920 despite Alf's objection that most local people did not want 'swanky' roads where working men could not afford to live: 'The whole idea is just a pet project of Councillor Cox's.'

The Sub-Committee rapidly began to achieve results. It pressurised the Corporation into agreeing to finance several initiatives designed to make serious inroads into the normally high winter levels of unemployment. Expenditure was approved for levelling the Pilot Field so that a proper sports ground could be laid out. The numbers of unemployed decorators were cut by the Council provision of indoor painting work. The Cemetery, its Church and Chapel, the Filsham and Brede Pumping Stations, Halton Fire Station and the Market Hall were redecorated.

But the Hastings Ratepayers' Association was aggrieved by this turn of events. The Corporation was surrendering to the 'forces of extravagance' and a 'squandermania disease'. This 'boiling sea of reckless and wasteful expenditure', as the press called it, brought the resignation of three town councillors in February 1921. Alf was delighted: his Sub-Committee motion was directly responsible. Others in the Council Chambers praised the departing councillors. The Mayor referred to the splendid work done by Councillor Mannington in his capacity as Chairman of the Finance Committee. Alderman Dighton also regretted his resignation; insisting the ratepayers had lost the services of one of the most valuable men he had known in all his twenty years' Council experience. Alf Cobb dissented: 'Councillor Mannington was the worst enemy of the working man; I am pleased he has resigned and hope more will do the same.'

Soon afterwards Councillor Fellows was elected as the new Mayor. After the formal ceremony was over Cobb withdrew, leaving the assembled Councillors and invited dignitaries to their luncheon entertainment. Sir Rider Haggard and Sir Henry Lunn were two of the guests that sat at the Mayor's table. Sir Henry toasted the Mayor and Corporation: 'It has been six years since I first had the honour of sitting at your festive board to meet the municipal fathers of this influential Borough.' Sir Rider then rose: 'I last spoke to this assembly in the very heart of War while the destinies of this Great Empire were being decided.' Heady stuff indeed!

The day before this great binge, the Council debated whether the Corporation should accept a tender for doorframes from outside the Borough, which undercut the lowest local tender by £300. Alf Cobb intervened: 'it is not the first time that people outside had realised the town was in a state of bankruptcy. By your trickery...' His speech was cut off by a furious Mayor who called the new Councillor severely to order: 'I will not have any member of this Council imputing base motives to other members.'

In that February of 1921, Hastings Magistrates sentenced an ex-serviceman to six months hard labour for obtaining dole money under false pretences. Mayor Fellows had been Chairman of the Borough Bench. The severity of the sentence was later raised in Council by Councillor Poynton: 'Six months for drawing unemployment pay whilst in work seems cruel for a first offence'. He understood an appeal had been made to the Home Secretary that might assist the Minister in lightening the sentence.

Mayor Fellows was in a delicate position. He tried to argue that the Council had no jurisdiction over a Treasury prosecution. Cobb begged to differ. He moved that the matter be considered at the meeting. The motion was ruled completely out of order. 'I must proceed to the next item,' insisted the Mayor. 'I refuse to accept your ruling,' answered Cobb,

> it is a matter of real and deep interest. Even if the whole story had been told, he could not have got a worse sentence. Look at the man's service overseas, where you did not go. Plenty of regiments would have been glad of your services.

'I don't care a rap what you say, Councillor Cobb. I only ask you to give me the civility and courtesy I extend to you.'

'I don't think you get anything else from me.'

A proposal that the Council should appeal to the Home Secretary was carried; a decision that undermined the Mayor's judgement and authority.

Alf Cobb made no attempt to hide his violent dislike of Fellows. His Worship equally loathed Alf. In all his too brief period as Councillor, Cobb openly demonstrated his contempt for official protocol and his scorn for the Mayor. At a Council sitting in March 1921, he was interrupted by the Mayor at question time.

'We cannot have a speech...'

'You sit down, Mr Mayor,' instructed Alf.

'You know who you are talking to, don't you? Don't tell me to sit down.'

Another Councillor intervened: 'I hope we are not in for an abusive afternoon; if so I'm going to retire.'

'I simply want to explain – uncomfortable though that is for some of you...'

Cobb was shouted down with cries of 'Order'. When he was finally allowed to speak he asked a series of searching questions about the Corporation contract with the Hastings Gas Company.

The Chief Constable had prepared a report on crime in the Borough for the year ending December 31st, 1920. After a member of the Watch Committee read out the report in Council, Alf stood up: 'Crime was manufactured by members of the Police Force, even to the extent of perjuring themselves in the witness box.' Amid loud exclamations of denial, the Mayor rose to confront Cobb, who remained standing.

'If you read your standing orders you will see a member should sit down when the Chairman stands up,' lectured Fellows.

'Very well, I'll sit down.'

He deliberately remained seated whilst moving a resolution that the

Corporation should forthwith dispose of the services of those constables guilty of crime – if necessary they should be replaced. The motion was lost. Two weeks later he moved the following resolution:

> That in the opinion of this Council the Electricity and Public Lighting Committee are deserving of severe censure in neglecting to discharge their duty in relation to the public lighting in various parts of the Borough.

He claimed that a woman resident had twice been robbed at night on the unlit path from Collier Road to Halton. He was accused of putting frivolous and vexatious motions on the agenda. This was probably the only time in the troubled history of Mugsborough's Council that a vote of censure was demanded because one particular street lamp remained unlighted.

One burning issue remained to confront the Corporation that day. The Borough Engineer's horse had grown old and lame. Last on the agenda was a written request by the officer; if he purchased a motor-car would the Council see its way clear to provide a chauffeur and pay fuel and running costs? Alf quickly moved that the Council reject the proposition: 'Why not have a bicycle?' he asked. The resolution was defeated. The horse was put down and a chauffeur was employed.

Chapter 21

Last Days

Alf Cobb's health was fast deteriorating. The wartime fall had caused permanent brain damage and the seizures and epileptic fits became steadily worse. His outbursts in Council, although fiery, lacked his usual sparkle and wit. He was too ill to attend the first Council meeting in April 1921. Mayor Fellows observed the usual formalities and asked the Town Clerk to despatch a letter of sympathy wishing him a speedy recovery. Alf was undergoing treatment at the Welsh Hospital, Netley.

A week before this letter of sympathy was drafted, an anonymous Corporation employee had corresponded with the Hastings' press. He described himself as a 'moderate trade unionist' who had not been persuaded to vote for the Socialist candidate by his workmates. He indicated that he had warned other Corporation staff that if Cobb were elected he would make a scene in Council – 'I have told them since I was right'. Alf kept abreast of the local news from his hospital bed. He had noted the reference to himself in the *Hastings Observer* and replied to the Editor:

> This proves the gentleman to be not only a great prophet, but a most accurate one. But a gentleman to hide himself behind his place of employment, I can well imagine to be in possession of other virtues than prophecy. It may even be possible to be particularly shy, not only as to name, but shy of work in the particular department he is engaged in. I wonder whether he has noticed the appointment of the Committee which will have to do with the reduction of bonuses, salaries and wages.
>
> I can promise him that Cobb, if recovered in time, will be present in the debate upon this matter and is fully prepared to make a scene if by so doing he can protect those workers, who really perform a useful duty to Hastings people, from a reduction of wages.

In Cobb's absence Councillors had engaged in a frantic search for economies. They had appointed a sub-committee in a bid to cut back the salaries of local officials by abandoning past bonuses and allowances.

Alf was discharged from hospital in time to attend a hastily arranged meeting on April 15th, organised by the Mayor, after the surprise resignation of the Town Clerk, Percy Idle. Idle had resolved to set up in private practice. His decision thoroughly alarmed Mayor Fellows. Without consulting his Councillor colleagues, he asked his Town Clerk to name a figure, which the town could afford, to make him 'a permanent and contented official'. Percy Idle had dithered but remained unmoved. He stated later that his resignation had not been aimed at raising his salary.

Cobb was the only Councillor not to express his regret at Percy Idle's departure. George Cox moved a resolution in a vain attempt to retain his services. Alf Cobb demurred: as a Corporation they had always to expect resignations, there were quite enough lawyers in Hastings to look after the people's interests. He thought that there were both better and worse solicitors; the position of Town Clerk was not one that a young man should have occupied during the War – the Council should proceed with electing a new Town Clerk. Despite Alf's protests, Cox had his way. A Committee was formed to interview Percy Idle and there was talk of a £1500 salary. It was all to no avail.

Although Cobb's health was failing, he rarely missed attending a Council meeting in the first summer months of 1921. By then he had only a short time to live. His illness was inflaming his mind. In June he was fined for striking a fourteen-year-old boy in the face. The lad worked at the Hastings railway station bookstall and had accidentally trodden on Alf's dog. Witnesses claimed that before the boy had a chance to explain that he had stepped back and caught the dog's foot, Alf had knocked him down, leaving him bleeding from swollen lips. Cobb's violent over-reaction was totally out of character. Annie Gannon describes him as a quietly spoken man who loved a joke: 'you never knew he had lost his temper, he always had a smile and greeting for everyone.'

Alf's last published letter was a response to a series of near-incoherent attacks against Frank Willard and himself by their passionate Conservative critic, the Reverend D. Henry Rees. His political misrepresentation caused a member of the same religious denomination to openly admit that he was ashamed to be associated with his colleague's position. Rees had written that Willard's and Cobb's style was 'a blend of truculence and bombast aimed at striking terror into the hearts of their opponents or at least leading their admiring followers to regard them as terrible fellows.' Below is part of Alf's long reply:

We have been fair to our reverends in our criticism of their teachings. We have our New Testament; we are able to prove that were Christ alive today He would be with us in the turning out of the money changers from the temple, and I have no doubt a large number of reverends with them...

A while ago Rees informed his readers he was journeying to the Downs. How funny; that is where the sheep are usually to be found. The Downs are beautifully green, but you must not expect all your readers to be so. Tomorrow I am journeying to a National Hospital, hoping to secure a real cure for disabilities obtained through national service... Please do be reasonable.

Willard's reply shows a typical religious and poetical strain:

The Socialist is not at all a nice man. He bawls unpleasant truths from the housetops; he forces upon the public mind the ghastly inequalities of our social system. The Socialist agitator of today merely does what an unlettered carpenter did more than nineteen centuries ago, and like Him he is faced with the hatred and enmity of the professors and preachers of his time; but though his feet may not tread the aisles of a church, nor his lips frame prayers which his heart does not inspire, he is often nearer in spirit to the meek and lowly Jesus than are those who worship Him with their lips, but who crucify Him daily by refusing social justice to their fellowmen...[51]

That summer a scheme to regulate the number of barrows and basket stands placed in the town's principal thoroughfares was finally approved. By an overwhelming majority, Councillors adopted the recommendations outlined in the Special Committee's concluding report. A compromise solution restricting the number of outdoor stands to specific public highways was ratified by both sides. It was backed by representatives of the Chamber of Trade and the Costermongers' Union. Twenty-five barrows were to be allowed to stand six feet from the footpath between the entrance to the Central Cricket Ground and the junction of South Terrace – a concession that later created a street market atmosphere in that section of Queen's Road. The scheme won the universal support of the local hawking fraternity. Cobb may have been too sick to witness the scheme's adoption by the Corporation but the costermongers knew that it was his tenacious leadership and stubborn defence of their rights that had played a major role in the settlement. His fame as the Hastings hawkers' champion spread far beyond the Borough Boundaries.

A month later Alf was dead. He had been admitted to hospital on many occasions after his army discharge but his condition proved untreatable. Always a fighter and ever the optimist, he never gave up hope of a cure to his suffering but in the weeks prior to his death, relatives had been informed there was no chance of a recovery.

Some local Socialists were convinced that once his identity was discovered his wartime injury was deliberately neglected but this is hard to take seriously after his lengthy service overseas. On Wednesday, August 31st, an ambulance brought him back to Hastings to spend his few remaining days at home. He died at his residence, 7 Brook Street, on Monday September 5th 1921, at the age of forty-seven. Annie Gannon sadly recalls how his mind would wander shortly before the end. In delirium he would begin to open a public address or chair a meeting. She can even remember him asking the phantom onlookers to make way to enable a little woman to see.

His many reactionary enemies rejoiced at his passing. A thorn in their tough hides had been removed. Officially the response was one of regret. Mayor Fellows suggested that the funeral should start at the steps of the Town Hall. Polly was vehemently opposed to this idea; fully aware it would have gone against Alf's wishes. She struggled unsuccessfully to discourage all official involvement in the ceremony; if the Mayor and his entourage must take part, then they could congregate at the Borough Cemetery – nothing more. Oblivious, the Mayor, wearing his chain of office, attended the funeral together with many other Council members, all deaf to the cry of 'hypocrite'. Even Chief Constable James, an old adversary, was present. Perhaps, looking back, some of these local functionaries secretly respected Alf's ability, his courage and irrepressible nature. Hundreds of people, including a large number of hawkers and ex-servicemen, followed the coffin to the grave.

Alf Cobb had a natural gift as an orator. His quick thinking and sharp wit never deserted him on a public platform. He was always able to wipe the floor with his rivals in debate. The sardonic, caustic humour, barbed repartee and cantankerous, tub-thumping style rarely failed to unnerve and disarm. It was a versatile talent. He could be blunt, abrasive and fearlessly outspoken but underneath lurked a keen sense of fun waiting to erupt.

He made sure, with a mulish perversity, that his was the last word on any issue; often carrying his argument to outrageous lengths long after his opponent had wilted. On many occasions local newspapers were compelled to foreclose on Cobb's fiercely argued correspondence. His political drive and contagious enthusiasm were fired by an unfaltering belief in a Socialist future. Within his lifetime, he would witness the triumph of municipal socialism in Hastings; of that he had no doubt. Politically self-taught, his capacity for hard work was legend amongst his Social Democratic colleagues.

He casually shrugged off the incessant vilification directed against him for his non-stop endeavour to overturn Mugsborough's rotten applecart, and committed his boundless energy to resolutely defending the cause of the political underdog; as the pages above testify. He was not known to have turned away a working man in trouble from his door. Annie Gannon can remember, as a child, Polly and Alf taking shifts to sit up all night nursing a sick neighbour.

It is difficult to assess the impact locally had Cobb lived into old age. Perhaps the other Councillors would have combined to outmanoeuvre him. But in his brief time as Councillor Cobb the Anti-Waste brigade was left rocking on its heels as the pressure to raise expenditure to reduce the numbers of unemployed ex-soldiers intensified and small public work schemes multiplied. A sudden settlement was also found to the long festering hawkers' dispute. A sleepy complacency returned to the town after his death; the Corporation breathed a collective sigh of relief.

Polly was heartbroken and devastated. She had been his devoted companion, lover and wife for twenty years. She survived her husband by just two years. She died at the East Sussex Hospital, after a serious operation, on Monday, October 8th, 1923. She was 46 years old. Alf's daughter from his first marriage 'Florrie', sang on the Hastings stage before emigrating to Canada in 1924.

Mary (Polly) Bassett lies buried beside Alf in the Borough Cemetery. The pauper's grave has no headstone. Two graves away is the elaborately carved gravestone of George Merryweather, Master of the Hastings Workhouse for twenty-one years. Alf Cobb would have appreciated the final irony.

Alf Cobb seeking votes during the council by-election, November 1910.

References

[1] *Hastings and St Leonards Observer,* 18th September, 1909

[2] Peak, S., (1985) *Fishermen of Hastings,* Newsbooks

[3] *Hastings Weekly Mail & Times,* October 20th 1906

[4] *Justice,* February 9th 1907

[5] *Hastings Weekly Mail & Times,* February 2nd 1907

[6] *Hastings Weekly Mail & Times,* February 9th 1907

[7] *Hastings Weekly Mail & Times,* February 9th 1909

[8] *Hastings Weekly Mail & Times,* March 2nd 1907

[9] *Justice* April 6th 1907

[10] *Hastings and St Leonards Observer,* August 10th 1907

[11] *Justice,* August 17th 1907

[12] *Hastings and St Leonards Observer,* September 7th 1907

[13] *Hastings and St Leonards Observer,* August 24th 1907

[14] *Hastings and St Leonards Observer,* September 21st 1907

[15] *Hastings and St Leonards Observer,* August 7th 1907

[16] *Hastings Weekly Mail and Times,* October 19th 1907

[17] *Hastings and St Leonards Advertiser,* October 24th 1907

[18] *Hastings and St Leonards Weekly Mail and Times,* February 5th 1908

[19] *Hastings and St Leonards Observer,* July 11th 1908

[20] *Hastings Weekly Mail and Times,* October 17th 1908

[21] G.D.H Cole and Raymond Postgate, *The Common People 1746–1946* (University Paperbacks, Methuen, London, p.428)

[22] Robert Tressell, *The Ragged Trousered Philanthropists,* London, Panther, p308

[23] *Hastings and St Leonards Observer,* June 19th 1909

[24] *Hastings and St Leonards Observer,* July 17th 1909

[25] *Hastings and St Leonards Observer,* November 13th 1909

[26] *Hastings and St Leonards Weekly Mail and Times,* January 29th 1910

[27] E.J. Hobsbawn (1964) *Labouring Men,* London, p.233

[28] *Hastings and St Leonards Weekly Mail and Times*, July 23rd 1910

[29] *Hastings and St Leonards Observer,* August 27th 1910

[30] *Justice,* October 8th 1910

[31] *Hastings and St Leonards Observer,* September 17th 1910

[32] *Justice,* October 15th 1910

[33] *Justice* October 29th 1910

[34] *Hastings and St Leonards Observer,* October 29th 1910

[35] *Justice,* November 12th 1910

[36] *Hastings Weekly Mail and Times,* November 5th 1910

[37] *Hastings and St Leonards Observer,* December 10th 1910

[38] *Hastings Weekly Mail and Times,* May 13th 1911

[39] *Hastings and St Leonards Observer,* July 15th 1911

[40] *Hastings and St Leonards Weekly Mail and Times,* July 22nd 1911

[41] *Hastings and St Leonards Observer,* July 22nd 1911

[42] *Justice* May 4th, 1912

[43] *Justice* August 17th 1912

[44] *Justice* September 7th 1912

[45] *Hastings and St Leonards Observer,* January 17th, 1914

[46] *Hastings and St Leonards Observer,* April 4th 1914

[47] *Hastings and St Leonards Observer,* August 22nd 1924.

[48] *Hastings and St Leonards Observer,* August 29th 1914.

[49] *Hastings and St Leonards Observer,* September 5th 1914

[50] *Hastings and St Leonards Observer,* December 14th 1918

[51] *Hastings and St Leonards Observer,* July 30th 1921

VICTORIAN WORKING WOMEN
A Study of Sussex

Helena Wojtczak

From boot-binders to brothel-keepers, from burglars to baby-killers, this groundbreaking book focuses on two aspects of women's lives rarely covered by historians: their paid work, and their involvement with the law. It also includes a broad overview of the social and legal status of women in Victorian England.

This fascinating book details the trials, tribulations and triumphs of women's lives in mid-19th century Sussex. Illustrated throughout with relevant Victorian advertisements and cartoons.

Price – to be advised.   Publishing date – autumn 2003.

RAILWAY WOMEN
The Story of a Forgotten Workforce

Helena Wojtczak

This book tells a tale of exploitation by the bosses, and of betrayal by the trades unions. It explains how women were utilised during two world wars and then discarded in peacetime, and describes the harassment experienced by the post-1975 recruits to traditionally male jobs. Ultimately, it is a story of triumph for, by the end of the book, women are represented in every railway occupation, and have equal opportunities and equal pay with men.

Price – to be advised.   Publishing date – late 2003.

THE DECLINE OF HASTINGS AS A SEASIDE RESORT

Mike Matthews

Price – to be advised.   Publishing date – late 2003.

THE HASTINGS PRESS
PO Box 96 Hastings TN34 1GQ
hastings.press @ virgin.net
Book orders: 01424 442 142